Scottish Ceramics

Henry E. Kelly

Schiffer Publishing Ltd
4880 Lower Valley Road, Atglen, PA 19310 USA

Photography by Douglas A. Leishman

Library of Congress Cataloging-in-Publication Data

Kelly, Henry E.
Scottish ceramics/Henry E. Kelly: photography by
Douglas A. Leishman.
p. cm.
ISBN 0-7643-0946-3 (hardcover)
1. Pottery, Scottish. I. Title.
NK4089.K45 1999
738'.09411--dc21 99-32124
CIP

Designed by Bonnie M. Hensley
Type set in Zapf Chancery Bd BT /Zapf Humanist 601 BT

ISBN: 0-7643-0946-3
Printed in China
1 2 3 4

Published by Schiffer Publishing Ltd.
4880 Lower Valley Road
Atglen, PA 19310
Phone: (610) 593-1777; Fax: (610) 593-2002
E-mail: Schifferbk@aol.com
Please visit our web site catalog at **www.schifferbooks.com**

In Europe, Schiffer books are distributed by Bushwood Books
6 Marksbury Avenue Kew Gardens
Surrey TW9 4JF England
Phone: 44 (0)181 392-8585; Fax: 44 (0)181 392-9876
E-mail: Bushwd@aol.com

This book may be purchased from the publisher.
Include $3.95 for shipping. Please try your bookstore first.
We are interested in hearing from authors with book ideas on related subjects.
You may write for a free printed catalog.

Acknowledgments

A book like this is not put together without a great deal of help from other people; collectors who have lent pieces for photography, scholars who have helped with advice or specialised knowledge, or just friends who have given time. I should like to express my gratitude to all of the following for the help they have given, without which this book could not have been put together: Douglas Bowie, June Clelland, Sandra Deas, Kate Downie, Michael and Marlene Egan, Len Fisher, George Fraser, Irene Graham, Marion Grant, Dr. J. Hendry, Heather Jack, George Kearney, Tina Kilgour, Barclay Lennie, Duncan and Helen McDonald, Hugh and Irene McIntyre, Liz McKelvie, Ian Menzies, William and Margaret More, Guy and Morag Pettigrew, William Rollo, Helen Sprott, Alice Watson and Margaret West. In the valuations of the pieces, the rate of exchange has been taken as $1.67 to the £. Of course, it varies from time to time and this must be taken into account.

Contents

1 Introduction

The history of the Scottish pottery industry extends over two hundred years but it is only in the last twenty years that it has been given any importance in the history of Scotland or of world ceramics.

While not rivaling the achievements of China or England in this field, the Scottish industry has yet made its mark in the creation of all kinds of ceramics from painted porcelain to bricks and stoneware which served the home market well and were exported all over the world. The export trade was always necessary since the home market was small and no Scottish pottery could hope to make much headway in England. The works of the Glasgow Pottery are greatly prized now by collectors in Malaysia and other areas of south-east Asia while Britannia and Bo'ness products are eagerly sought after in Canada. Spongeware from Scotland seems to be collectible all over the world, from the U.S.A. to Borneo.

The industry spread over the whole of the central Scottish belt but concentrated in five main areas. Most important was Glasgow and its surroundings which had by far the largest number of potteries of all kinds but Greenock, Bo'ness, Kirkcaldy and the coastal area of East Lothian had their importance. These centres had most of the whiteware potteries but redware potteries were widely scattered from Aberdeen to Ayrshire, though in much smaller numbers than in England or Wales. Fireclay potteries and brickworks existed wherever there was coal-mining, e.g. in north Lanarkshire in Fife and in north Ayrshire.

The classic text on the subject is *Scottish Pottery* by J.Arnold Fleming (Glasgow 1923). This is now rather scarce as is a reprint published in the 1970s. Arnold Fleming owned the Britannia Pottery and worked in the industry for some years; his evidence is largely verbal and anecdotal so, although his book is gripping, full of information and essential as a source, it is unreliable and all information must be checked. In the reading list given for each pottery it should always be understood that Fleming's book is included in the list and the relevant chapter should be read if possible.

Scottish East Coast Potteries 1750-1840 by Patrick McVeigh is crammed with lovely illustrations. Unfortunately the attributions and dating rely solely on unsupported opinion, making the book very misleading. It should nevertheless be taken as a source for the history of potteries in East Lothian.

Apart from these two texts, the only other general work of any depth is the research published by the Scottish Pottery Society in its journal — *Scottish Pottery Historical Review* (SPHR). This has now run to nineteen numbers. There are many booklets and papers scattered in the literature and they are given in the reading list for each chapter.

In the text which follows each pottery has been given a chapter with a brief history of the works and a discussion of the wares with illustrations. To this is appended a reading list and a resume of the pottery descriptions. The expression 'pottery descriptions' is used rather than backstamps or marks since it is unusual for a Scottish pottery to have a mark in the sense in which this is used in some other countries. The custom with transfer printed marks in Scotland is to have a separate backstamp for each pattern. With this goes a pottery description usually in the form of the owner's name or the initials of the firm's name (e.g. COCHRAN or J. &. M.P.B. & Co.). This may change without changing the backstamp otherwise (e.g. R. COCHRAN & Co. or J. & M.P.B. & Co.Ld.) More extreme examples are known than the ones quoted. The pottery descriptions are usually used throughout a series of backstamps and it can be seen from this that they are of greater importance than the actual backstamps in understanding the history of the pottery. Moreover, listing the number of known backstamps would mean devoting an enormous space to each pottery, enough to fill several volumes. Examples of backstamps are given for many potteries. As so often occurs, Bells' Pottery is the exception. Their JB in a bell impressed is used on an enormous range of wares, often with no other mark. For instance it was used for many years as the only mark on porcelain or parian until, in 1881, it was partially replaced by a B in a bell.

All of the most important Scottish potteries are included. Some of the smaller and more ephemeral whiteware potteries have been excluded, especially some early ones where no wares have been identified. Some of these can be studied through G. Quail's *Four Early Glasgow Potteries* (Glasgow 1982) or in works recommended in the reading lists. Many redware potteries have not been included for much the same reason since very little is known of them or their products.

The pattern lists given with each entry reflect the present state of knowledge and are subject to change and correction always. Several new patterns have been made known to the author by chance or by the kindness of individuals while this book was being written. There is a small glossary at the end of the text to help with words and phrases which may be unfamiliar to the reader. The terms used by collectors in the U.S.A. and the United Kingdom are so different that it is easy for misunderstandings to occur.

An inevitable omission is the enormous bulk of early ware which cannot be attributed to any pottery with any certainty. Little potteries sprang up around Glasgow or on the banks of the Forth and made a little creamware which, like most of the bigger potteries, they did not mark, perhaps because they hoped it would be mistaken for Wedgwood's. Black basalte was almost never marked in Scotland and can only be distinguished from English ware by the fact that the Scots pieces have a lick of glaze on the outside (1.1). Just for interest there is also a photograph of some ware made at Barvas on the Isle of Lewis in this century for sale to tourists. The Highland tradition of pottery making goes back for thousands of years and the wares were of excellent quality but those shown here were made in imitation of commercial wares of the time. The result is distinctly odd (1.2).

1.1. Two creamware porringers: one with whistle handle, 4.5" diam., 2.75" ht., and 5" diam., 3" ht.(£100/$170 - £200/$340). Black basalte teapot, 6" ht.(£70/$120).

1.2. Three pieces of Barvas ware from the Isle of Lewis (£30-90/$50-150). Teapot, 5.75" ht. Cup, 2.5" ht. Craggan, 3.5" ht.

2

Alloa Pottery, Alloa

This Pottery was founded c.1783 in Kirkgate, Alloa, by James Shaw—known as Sheepy Shaw—to make common redware. It rapidly passed through the hands of a number of owners: James Turnbull (until 1805), James Heath (1812-16), William Hamilton and William Gardner (c.1820-1856).

Gardner was a son of Peter Gardner of Dunmore Pottery and himself an experienced potter, having been trained in Glasgow in all aspects of the manufacture of whiteware. Under his rule the pottery produced not only Rockingham glazed wares but majolica wares and white and cane-coloured earthenware and above all jet. However, in 1856 William Gardner & Son went bankrupt and the pottery was purchased shortly thereafter by Joseph Bailey, an Edinburgh china retailer. From now until its closure the pottery was owned and run by the Bailey family.

Output was increased under the new owners and showrooms opened in London and Bristol, a habit at this time of all the major potteries in Scotland. But Alloa Pottery was not without its troubles. In the late 1880s a dispute arose with the makers of teapots, the major output of the pottery. The Baileys were paying their men at a lesser rate than the Glasgow and English potteries and would not fall into line. Several of the men left without giving proper notice; workers were recruited from Staffordshire to replace them but when they found out the true rate of pay they too left. The Baileys pursued those who had left in both the Scottish and English courts of law and in general won £5 in damages from each man. But even so the days of the pottery were numbered and foreign competition was causing the loss of orders. So when deaths occurred in the Bailey family, the Works was closed down in 1907.

Attribution of pieces to Alloa Pottery has many problems since many of their products were not marked. A certain amount of research has eased the problem but the issue has been confused also by a large number of unsupported attributions over the years. The problem is particularly difficult with jetware teapots since they seem to have been very seldom marked. The absence of marks means also that many attributions are subject to reservations and qualifications.

The vast majority of the output has been in jet, Rockingham and majolica wares. The former two seem overwhelmingly to have been teapots, though pitchers, spittoons, kettles, flower pots, fern pots, sugars, creams, butter dishes, etc. were also made.

Other colored wares seem to have played a lesser part though imitations of Cumnock motto ware were made for Shearer, a Glasgow dealer. Whiteware played a very minor part in the output.

Pottery Descriptions: impressed or printed

W. & J.A. Bailey

W. & J.A.B.Alloa

Reading: Spreull, Professor James A. S. and Robert Rankine. *Alloa Pottery*. Clackmannan District Libraries, 1993.

Patterns:

Since very little whiteware was made and since most decoration was by painting, the Alloa Pottery has no named transfer patterns.

Pine Apple — a rare named, moulded pattern.

2.1. Two moulded teapots with Chinese scene and Rockingham glaze, 9" ht. £50/$85 each.

2.2. Pitchers: Pine Apple, 8" ht. (£45/$75), splash glaze and moulded shell and anchor, 6.75" ht.(£40/$70), mazarin blue glaze, 6" ht. (£40/$70). Dish marked SHEARER GLASGOW (£25/$40).

2.3. Tea kettle with majolica glazes (£100/$170).

2.4. Pitcher, 6.75" ht. and teapot with Rockingham glaze. Splash glazed plate. £40/$70 each.

2.5. Pair of majolica glazed pitchers, 7" ht. (£40/$70 the pair)

3

Annfield Pottery, Glasgow

Annfield Pottery, named after the estate on which it was built, was the largest whiteware pottery in Glasgow's east end. The date of establishment is given variously as about 1816 and 1826. The founder was John Thomson, a Glaswegian who is said to have brought his potters from Burslem in north Staffordshire.

The pottery was built on old-fashioned lines judging by the submissions to the Royal Commission (on the employment of children) of 1862, which are the gloomiest of all given by Scottish potteries. There is even a claim that all potters suffer an early death due to their trade. Similar submissions from Bells' and Victoria Potteries are much more optimistic and deny that potters are short-lived. By 1865 Thomson's three sons had been taken into partnership and, after John Thomson's death in 1873 they ran the business until the 1880s. The date of closure is slightly doubtful; the Works were closed by 1883 but the business was not finally wound up until 1887.

Not much work has been done on the products of Annfield Pottery but a timely reminder of the partial state of our knowledge was lately given by a report of the finding of sherds from the pottery in a military latrine in Canada dating from between 1843 and 1854. These include painted wares, spatter ware and children's plates, all pieces which are rarely marked and therefore rarely attributed to specific potteries. As well as this, Annfield is known to have made spongeware throughout its life.

According to Fleming, Annfield was famous for mulberry wares in its early years and Royal Rose (3.1) is certainly evidence of this. Cynthia has been reported from the U.S.A. but not from Britain and comes from a surprisingly late date. Voilet (3.2) is halfway towards a true purple while Sydney (3.3) sometimes shows the difficulties with the initial stages of this color. It was also used as a dinner ware pattern. Athenian (3.2) appears in blue and black and Wellington (3.4) in a blue/green. Thereafter all transfer colors are used.

Dinner ware patterns Castle and Watteau were also found in Canada while Grecian (3.5) is the standard lacustrine landscape for the pottery. Prince of Wales has been found on only one dinner service with an inscription included in the pattern. This reads: AS A SMALL TRIBUTE OF RESPECT TO THE MEMORY OF THE LATE MR. SAMUEL COULTERS, OF THIS CITY THIS SERVICE IS PRESENTED TO THE SURVIVING MEMBERS OF HIS FAMILY BY JOHN THOMSON ANNFIELD POTTERY GLASGOW 1842. Samuel Coulters (or Coulter) was a house and sign painter; the gift was regal (3.3).

Other dinner ware patterns include Marine Grotto, Peacock, Indostan (a changing pattern) and Chariot (3.4, 6). Willow was made with a unique mark (3.7). Andalusia (3.8) was used on dinner ware, tea ware and porringers, while Persian (3.9) and other patterns (3.10) were used exclusively on porringers. Sydenham, with the unique pottery description I.T., appeared only on bedroom ware, so far as we know (3.11).

Fleming states that John Thomson's wares found a very successful market in Australia but this has yet to be confirmed from that continent itself. A few pieces have been found in Java but not enough to register more than an emigrant's household goods.

At a slightly later date Fern, Water Lily and Caledonia were popular pitcher patterns (3.12) though others have been found (3.13). Cable was used for dinner wares (3.11).

After John Thomson retired, the wares definitely declined in quality both in body and in design. Athena for pitchers (3.15) was a poor copy of Sydney. Chalons, Statuettes and Shanghai (3.16, 17) appeared on pitchers, though in the last example it might have been better not to. Chantilley and Provence (3.15) are copies of Bells' patterns while Pekin (on tea ware) is simply Bells' Tamerlaine renamed. Presumably they bought the copper plates from Bell. Labyrinth was a standard dinner ware pattern all through the pottery's life.(3.19).

No purely ornamental wares have ever been found from Annfield Pottery; it was a strictly utilitarian Pottery which in its early years produced pieces of good quality.

Pottery Descriptions: Thomson — impressed
J.T. — printed
Prince of Wales — printed
J.T. & Sons

Reading: Kelly, H.E. "The marked jugs of the Annfield Pottery" in *SPHR* 15 (1993): 87-94.
______. "Annfield Jugs Revisited" in *SPHR* 16 (1994): 71.
______. "The Royal Commission on the Employment of Children" in *SPHR* 16 (1994): 38-43.
Quail, G. "The Annfield Pottery" in *SPHR* 8 (1984): 32-39.
Sussman, Lynne. "John Thomson's Wares found at a Canadian Site" in *SPHR* 17 (1995): 7-13.

Pattern List:

J.T. period:

Albert — a mourning pattern for Prince Albert.
Alma — terrace with urn
Alpine Sports — boys raiding an eagle's nest
Andalusia
Asiatic Pheasant — the usual pattern.
Athenian
Brigand — lacustrine landscape with two armed men sitting on a rock.
Cable
Caledonia
Castle
Cavendish
Chariot
Corsina
Crest
Crown — three allegorical figures, one being crowned.
Fawn — girl with fawn
Fern
Flora — a man and a woman seated in a landscape
Flora's Gems or Floral Gems
Free Trade
Grecian
Indostan
Ivanhoe — a scene from the novel
Juvenile Companions — boy and girl catching butterflies
Labyrinth
Marine Grotto
Oriental — eastern scene with camel
Palm — oriental scene with figures
Peacock
Persian
Prince of Wales
Royal Rose
Sydenham
Sydney
Tyrol — two girls with goats in a landscape with a chalet
Voilet
Water Lily
Watteau
Wellington
Wild Rose — the usual pattern
Willow — the usual pattern

J.T. & Sons period:

Alhambra — returned from Java
Apple
Asiatic Pheasants — the usual pattern
Athena
Aurora — angels, dated 1871 or 4.
Autumnal — a thick band of leaves
Birds — birds.

3.1. Royal Rose. Porringer, 6" diam. (£40/$70). Pitchers, 8" ht. (£50/$85 each).

3.2. Porringer: Voilet, 6" diam.(£40/$70). Pitchers: Athenian, 6" and 8" ht. (£35, 60/$60, 100).

Bordeaux — shelf with fruit and baskets
Chalons
Chantilley — sometimes spelt Chantilly.
Cynthia — a lacustrine landscape with a vase on a balustrade.
Delhi — identical to Clyde Pottery's pattern — this came back from Java.
Dunoon — scrolls and foliage
Flora
Hong Kong
Labyrinth
Lelia
Maltese
Neva — returned from Java — may be an earlier piece.
Pekin
Provence
Shanghai
Statuettes
Thionville.

3.4. Pitcher: Wellington, 8.5" ht. (£180/$300). Plates: Marine Grotto, 9.5" diam. Peacock, 11" diam. (£35/$60 each).

3.3. Plate: Prince of Wales, 10" diam.(£40/$70). Pitchers: Sydney, 8.75" (£40/$70 each).

3.5. Plates: back — Grecian, 9.5" diam.(£25/$60) — front — Castle, 9.5" diam.(£30/$50), Watteau, 11" diam. (£35/$60).

3.6. Indostan Plate, 9.5" diam.(£35/$60) and sauceboat, 5" ht.(£30/$50). Chariot Plate, 10.5" ht. (£35/$60).

3.7. Willow mark.

3.8. Andalusia, 8" and 10.5" diam. (£35/$60 each).

3.9. Persian, 6" diam. (£45/$75).

3.10. Unnamed porringer, 6" diam. (£45/$75).

3.11 Royal Rose, Sydenham. The soap dish is unmarked and may not be by Annfield. Soap dish, 5" lgth. (£30/$50). Ewer, 12.25"ht. (£70/$120).

3.12. Pitchers: Fern, 8" ht. (£35/$60), Caledonia, 8.25" ht. (£35/$60).

3.13. Unnamed pattern (£50/$85).

3.14. Ashet: Cable, 11" lgth. (£20/$35).

3.15. Pitchers: Athena, 8.75" ht. Porringers: back — Provence, 6" diam. — front — Chantilley, 6" diam. (£35/$60 each).

3.16. Pitchers: Chalons, 7.5" ht.(£40/$70), Water Lily, 7" ht. (£50/$85), Shanghai, 8" ht. (£50/$85).

3.17. Pitcher: Statuettes, 7.75" ht.(£50/$85).

3.18. Tea plate: Pekin, 8" diam. (£25/$40).

3.19. Ashet: Labyrinth, 11.5" lgth. (£25/$40).

3.20. Pitcher: Thionville, 7" ht. (£60/$100).

4

Barrowfield Pottery, Glasgow

Henry Kennedy, founder of the Barrowfield Pottery, came from Ireland to Glasgow at an unknown date before 1856 and from an unknown place. His father is known to have been a farmer and grocer but nothing more has been found out. Henry is said to have worked at the St. Rollox Flax Mill and, in 1856, to have moved to the nearby Caledonian Pottery of the Murray family, yet three years later he married Mary Barbour, daughter of the owner of St. Rollox Flax Mill.

In 1866, dissatisfied with his progress under the Murrays, he left to found the Barrowfield Pottery in Glasgow's east end. At first this was a small concern, making stonewares with a single kiln; only the plainest and most utilitarian wares were made. But Kennedy was a very astute businessman and the following years find him buying more land to extend his premises and by 1872 paying off his debts. In October 1876 he was rich enough to lend £14900 to a builder and by 1878 was lending £2550 to a surgeon. Both of these are considerable sums of money at that date. Over the years the pottery expanded and by 1896 had eighteen kilns.

We have a complete description of the pottery from a journal of 1880 which mentions eight kilns and clay from Devon being bought in sufficient quantities to last over the winter months. The works seem to have been fully mechanised by steam power, including the turning of the wheels. The pottery is credited with making 1530 dozen bottles per day and these are hand-thrown rather than moulded. The saggers are made on the premises from clay from Garnkirk and Glenboig, near Glasgow. As many as 600 a week are made.

Around 1881 Kennedy's sons, Joseph and John, joined the business which changed its name to Henry Kennedy & Sons and from this date Kennedy took a lesser part in running the firm. In April 1884 there was a disastrous fire when the heat of the kilns ignited the woodwork and £5000 of damage was done and another in 1888 but neither seems to have permanently injured the business. Kennedy died on 14 July 1890 of a brain lesion (a stroke?). Before 1896 John left the business to found the much smaller Cleland Pottery in Lanarkshire and Joseph carried on as Henry Kennedy & Sons Ltd. until 1929 when the pottery finally closed down.

Some photographs taken in the 1920s, probably of this pottery, exist.

The business was very quickly successful and as this occurred more ornamental wares were added to the repertoire. Whisky flasks were produced with impressed and printed designs in black and usually some iron wash on the neck or neck and shoulders. Designs include hawthorn blossom, deer and scenes from Burns' poems. A moulded hexagonal salt bucket covered in white slip decorated in blue and brown and with a bearded head on the front has been attributed to the Pottery. Later they experimented with agate ware in blue, white, brown and grey. Yellow ware for kitchen use was produced and brown teapots, both under the punning title 'Delaware' and with a native American head in full headdress as a trade mark. The most frequently found pieces of ornamental ware are, however, tobacco and snuff jars in various shapes with moulded busts of smoking men and snuff-taking women.

The Barrowfield Pottery is amongst the small group known to have made beer bottles for breweries in various South American countries, e.g. Argentina, Uruguay and Chile.

Pottery Descriptions: Henry Kennedy
Henry Kennedy & Sons (Ltd.)
Delaware — all impressed.

Reading: "Barrowfield Pottery" in *The Mercantile Age* for 18 May 1880.
Quail, G. "The Barrowfield Pottery" in *SPHR 10* (1986): 16-21 [care is needed; this has inaccuracies].

4.1. Butter jar, 5.25" ht. with retailer's name and address (£45/$75); small pitcher (£45/$75); whisky jug (£35/$60). The last two with iron wash on the upper parts.

4.2. Jam jars for 1 lb. and 2 lb.(£15/$25 each); pneumatic trough with retailer's name and address (£45/$75). The latter was used for collecting gases made from chemical reactions.

4.3. Electrical insulator (damaged), 4" lgth. (£5/$8).

4.4. Whisky flagons with hawthorn prints (£50/$85) and scene from Tam O'Shanter (£90/$150), all 8" ht.

4.5. Cream jar with retailer's name and address (£20/$35); whisky flagons, one with scene from Tam O'Shanter (£90/$150).

4.6. Agate ware vase, 6" ht. (£60/$100) and jardiniere, 6.25" ht. (£90/$150).

4.7. Rockingham glazed teapots, 7.25" and 8.5" ht. (£45/$75 each).

4.8. Mark on one of the 4.7 teapots.

5

Belfield's Pottery, Prestonpans

This Pottery, at the west end of Prestonpans in East Lothian, was founded—probably in 1837—by Charles Belfield, a potter and son of another potter. In 1837 he would be about 48 years of age and was married with three sons who also trained as potters. It is possible that the family was originally English and had been involved in nearby Cousland Pottery, a small works whose history is not well known.

At first the business was small, probably only a family concern, but it was successful and gradually expanded. In the Census of 1871 Belfield is shown as employing 27 men and 13 boys.

Charles Belfield senior died in 1850 of 'water on the chest', leaving his two surviving sons, Charles and James, to run the business. James died in 1878, leaving no children and the pottery was in the hands of Charles and three of his seven sons, Charles junior, Frank and John. Charles senior died in 1890 closely followed by Frank in 1892. The last of the family to survive, John Clark Belfield, died in 1941 but it is probable that the pottery had closed in the early 1930s.

The premises stood till the 1970s when everything was demolished. Photographs of the works taken just previous to demolition exist.

Belfield's specialised in coloured wares: brown teapots (sometimes moulded as bamboo), green leaf-moulded dessert plates, mazarin blue tea and water pots, and splash-glazed wares are the best known products. However, during excavation whiteware sherds were found which had been previously unknown from this source.

Belfield's production seems to have consisted mainly of Rockingham glazed teapots and majolica wares. The latter can be hard to identify since, like Alloa's, they were seldom marked and the quality was about the same as Alloa's. Mazarin blue was a less frequent product.

Pottery Description: Belfield & Co.

Reading: McDonald, Irene. "Closure of Belfield's and More on Belfield's" in *Scottish Pottery Society Archive News* 2 (1977): 5-6

Dalgleish, Robert at al. *Pots at the Pans* (Newtongrange 1990)

5.1. Rockingham glazed teapot moulded as bamboo, 8" ht. (£60/$100); two unmarked majolica pitchers, 5.75" and 7" ht. (£35/$60).

5.2. Rockingham glazed teapot of smaller size, approx. 5" ht. (£70/$120).

5.3. Mark on the Rockingham glazed teapot seen in 5.2.

5.4. Teapot, 5.25" ht. and coffee pot or water jug, 6.5" ht. in mazarin blue (£35/$60 each).

5.5. Newhaven fishwives. These figures are unmarked but are traditionally attributed to Belfield's Pottery; however, there is a rival attribution to Prestonpans, giving a very different date (£90/$150).

6

Bo'ness Pottery, Bo'ness

The Bo'ness Pottery was founded c.1766 in Bo'ness, a prosperous port on the south bank of the River Forth, near the site of the east end of the Antonine Wall. Originally coarse redware was made but very quickly clay was imported from England to make creamware and white earthenware. The founder was Dr. John Roebuck, a pivotal figure in the development of industry in east central Scotland. He was a partner in the Carron Iron Works and owner of a sulphuric acid plant in Prestonpans; coal-mining and salt making were among his interests and he was an early employer of James Watt whose job was to stop flooding in Roebuck's mines. By the time of his death in 1791, forty men, boys and girls were employed.

After this the pottery was run briefly by one John Cowan who sold it in 1799 to Alexander Cumming. Alexander Cumming was succeeded by his nephew James C. Cumming. His ownership was followed by a mysterious period in which the family Shaw were owners, perhaps in trust for a relation by marriage, James Jamieson.

In 1826, James Jamieson took over the Company which traded as J. Jamieson & Co. Jamieson died in 1829 and his infant son inherited the pottery which was run by members of the family. The Works were greatly extended. Wares from this period are well known and of quite a high quality. Earthenware was made, decorated mostly with transfer prints but sometimes with sponge-printing. Jamieson died in 1859 and the pottery was bought by John Marshall, Jamieson's brother-in-law.

The trading name was now J. Marshall & Co. The wares made were of much the same type but the quality was not quite so high, though the pottery traded successfully. Wares were exported, particularly to Canada and Ireland. William McNay, who was the works' traveler, was taken on as a partner; but, the deaths of Marshall and McNay in 1879 and 1880 respectively were blows from which the pottery never really recovered. It traded for a short time as John Marshall & Co. Ltd. but then closed down finally.

The earliest piece which can be attributed to the Bo'ness Pottery is a redware flask or bottle. It is covered with white slip and sgraffito decorated overall with stab marks. On one side also is the picture of a sailing ship and on the opposite I.P. and 1794. The initials probably stand for John Paris and the flask descended through the family until very recent years. The Paris family was involved in the pottery trade in both Greenock and Bo'ness (6.1, 2).

The wares of the Jamieson period are mostly transfer printed though it is known from excavation that spongeware of a primitive type was made very soon after its introduction. It was normally unmarked and therefore unidentifiable. The transfer prints were of good quality and seldom clobbered. Modern Athens was a changing pattern with views of Edinburgh (6.3, 4). It was during this time that Bo'ness' stock pattern was introduced in the form of Bosphorus, a lacustrine landscape (6.5, 10). This pattern was used for dinner ware and other shapes over a fairly long period of time by several potteries in the north of England as well as in eastern Scotland. Asiatic Flowers sees not to have been such a success since it is now much scarcer (6.5, 7, 8). Canton (6.5) is an oddity, a moulded pitcher with a pattern name. It carries an impressed mark and is found with and without a Britannia metal lid and with or without a strainer at the spout. Falconry (6.9, 13) has been found on pitchers as well as punchbowls. Royal Vase (6.10) is sometimes found on pitchers almost large enough to be a ewer. California and Rose are other pitcher patterns (6.12).

Dinner ware patterns include Forth and Swiss Scenery (6.11). Australia is a fairly rare dinner ware pattern (6.13) with a slight puzzle attached to it. Besides the obvious original Australia, there is a sheet pattern so marked by the pottery (6.14, 27). The most obvious reason for the use of the same mark on the second pattern is that this was bought in (purchased from an outside source) and came with no mark, so the mark from a not very popular pattern was used up on this new design. It seems unlikely that the Works would have run two patterns simultaneously which had the same name and mark. Rajah was an exotic pattern with elephants (6.14). Other dinner ware patterns include Coral, Florentine

Villas and another sheet pattern with leaves and flowers and the word FREE (6.15, 16). This last was used also by Victoria Pottery and probably by Britannia.

Tea ware was made with Triumphal Car (6.11) and Wellington (6.15). The former was a variant on Bells' pattern, the latter a commemorative for the Duke of Wellington's death.

The pottery description B.P.Co. undoubtedly belongs to Bo'ness Pottery but its date seems to be in some doubt. It was possibly used in the early part of the Jamieson ownership but could have been used at the latter end of the same period. It is found on porringers with Goat and on plates with Asiatic Pheasant (6.17, 18).

In the Marshall period, clobbering on patterns became more common but the quality of the ware varied much more than under the Jamiesons. Pitcher patterns which are more or less clobbered include Venice (6.19, 20), Cupid (6.21) and Birds (6.22) and Robin, which is a Christmas pitcher (6.23). Another set of pitchers carries the same emblems of the months as Bells' do but much more carelessly engraved (6.21). Other pitchers include Band of Hope (6.22) and a moulded shape with a mask (6.24) in imitation of a shape made by Clyde Pottery. There is a series of jugs with black transfers on top of a pink ground (6.25). Patterns seen include a sailor, a commemorative for the Glasgow International Exhibition of 1888 and an engraving called The Turk.

Dinner wares are found with Cable (6.25) and Tonkin (6.24) which are also found on pitchers. H. M. Stanley seems to be meant as a wall plaque rather than a plate but there seem to be more than one pattern featuring Stanley (6.23, 26). Levana is an angel pattern of the type very popular in the 1870s. There is also an octagonal wall plaque commemorating the 1888 Glasgow Exhibition.

There was certainly an export trade with Ireland and Canada and the firm indeed produced a special changing pattern for the latter market known as Canadian Sports (6.22). The scenes in this are rarely found in Britain but are well documented, being found quite commonly in the country for which they were destined.

In the later part of its life Bo'ness produced 'breakfast sets' comprising a mug, a porringer and a creamer. These sets are now seldom found complete but Horse Shoe seems to have been a common pattern for this use (6.19). Latterly also pitchers were produced in different shapes (6.27).

Bo'ness never made porcelain or grand exhibition pieces to our knowledge but for most of its life it made excellent serviceable everyday wares.

Pottery Descriptions: all printed

J.J. — J.J. & Co. (occasionally impressed)
J.Jamieson & Co.
J.M. & Co.
J.Marshall & Co.
B.P.Co.

Reading: Bowie, Douglas. "Bo'ness Sheet Patterns" in *SPHR* 8 (1984): 28-31.
Quail, G. "Bo'ness Patterns" in *SPHR* 9 (1985): 54.
Roberts, Christine & Lyon, Beverly 'Bo'ness Potteries' Falkirk Museum 1977.

Pattern List:

Jamieson period:

Asiatic Flowers
Asiatic Pheasant
Australia
"Australia"
Bosphorus
California
Canton
Coral
Falconry
Florentine Villas
Forth
Fountain
Goat
Gothic
Hawthorn Blossom
Modern Athens
Rajah
Rose
Royal Vase
Triumphal Car
Victoria

6.1, 2. Flask: red ware with white slip and sgraffito decoration — 1794, approx. 7" ht. — priceless.

Wellington.

Marshall period: Many of these come from a catalogue for the sale of plant and machinery at the close down in 1899. Some of them are not known from any other source.

Albert — dinner ware.
Alexandra — tea ware.
Autumn — tea ware and pitchers — dinner ware.
Bathurst — spray pattern.
Band of Hope
Birds
Bosphorus
Bramble
Broseley
Cable
Cairo — tea ware.
Canadian Sports
Cattle — mug and bowl.
Chily
Cupid
Donkey — bowl, cream and mug.
Dr. Jim — plates.
Duke and Duchess of York
Elfin — pitcher.
Excelsior — dinner ware.
Fern — toilet ware, flower pots, cheese stands, etc.
Glasgow — a border of fan shapes — almost identical to a Bells' export pattern — tea ware.
Grecian — the usual grey pattern — dinner ware.
Greek — dinner ware.
Harp — bowl, cream and mug.
Heron — plates.
H. M. Stanley
Hop — hops.
Horse Shoe
Indian Group — toilet.
I'se Biggest — girl and dog — punch bowl, bowl, cream and mug.
Jarra — tea ware.
Killarney — set of jug plates (?).
Lachine — a floral border pattern — dinner and toilet ware.
Levana
Lily — tea ware.
Lothian — set of jug plates (?)
Madeira
Madrid — dinner ware pattern.
Mayflower — border pattern cut for American market, will print dinner ware and tea ware.
Paris
Parma — dinner ware, etc.
Pheasant
Poppy — bowl, cream and mug.
Prince of Wales — toilet set.
Rhine — dinner ware.
Rhodes — plates.
Robin
Rural — various animals and vehicles.
Sandhurst — stylised formal pattern — dinner, tea, toilet sets, flower pots, cheese stand etc.
Sprig
Stanley — border pattern, cut for American market — tea and dinner ware.
Strand — floral border pattern — tea and dinner ware.
Sunflower — bowl, cream and mug.
Tonkin
The Turk — a Turkish soldier on horseback.
Turkish — mug and can.
Venice — tea ware.
Victoria — toilet set.
Willow — dinner ware.
Wolseley — portrait of Sir Garnet Wolseley.
York — toilet set.

6.3, 4. Modern Athens in various colors and shapes. Underdish (£50/$85); serving dish (£80/$135); ashet (£180/$300); bowl (£100/$170); plate (£65/$110); tea plate (£50/$85).

6.5. Plates: Bosphorus, 10" diam.(£25/$40). Pitchers: Canton (moulded), 6.5" ht. and Asiatic Flowers, 8.5" ht. (£90/$150).

6.6. Bosphorus mark.

6.7. Punch bowl: Asiatic Flowers (£90/$150).

6.8. Asiatic Flowers mark.

6.9. Punch bowls: Falconry (£60/$100).

6.10. Punch bowl: Bosphorus (£50/$85). Pitchers: Falconry, 8" ht. (£50/$85) and Royal Vase, 9.5" ht.(£85/$140). Double spouted teapot: Bosphorus (undamaged £150/$250).

6.11. Tea plate: Triumphal Car, approx. 7" diam.(£30/$50). Plates: Forth and Swiss Scenery (£40/$70 each).

6.12. Pitchers: California (£80/$135), Royal Vase, Rose (£60/$100), approx. 8" ht. each.

6.13. Pitchers: Falconry, 8.25" ht. (£35-60/$60-100). Plate: Australia, 10.5" diam.(£60/$100).

6.14. Plate: Rajah, approx. 9" diam.(£35/$60). Bowl (£35/$60), cup and saucer (£40/$70) with "Australia."

6.15. Tea plate: Wellington (£60/$100). Plates: Florentine Villas (£45/$75) and "Free" (£35/$60).

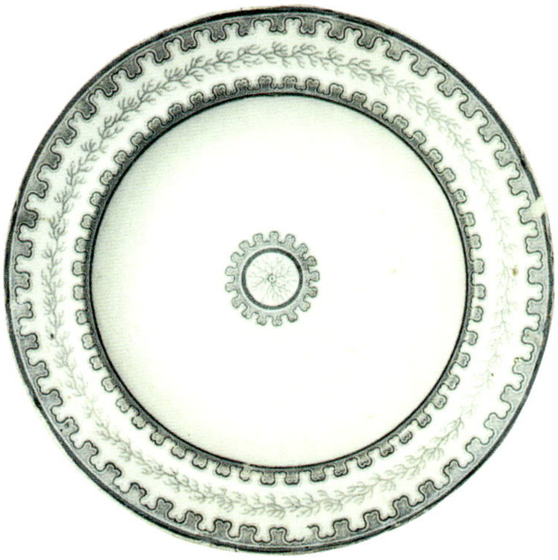

6.16. Plate: Coral, approx. 10" diam. (£40/$70).

6.17. Bowls: Goat, 7" diam.(£35, 40/$60, 70). Plate Asiatic Pheasant, approx. 9.25" diam. (£20/$35).

6.18. Mark on bowl in 6.17.

6.19. Pitcher: Venice, 8" ht. (£60/$100). Horse Shoe mug, 4" ht. (£40/$70) and porringer, 5.25" diam. (£35/$60).

6.20. Venice mark.

6.21. Bowl: Levana (£40/$70). Pitchers: Cupid, 7.25" ht. (£70/$120), the months, 8" ht. (£60/$100).

6.22. Teapot: Canadian Sports (£120/$200). Pitchers: Birds, 8" ht.(£50/$85), Band of Hope, 8" ht. (£70/$120).

6.23. Pitcher: Robin, 7.5" ht. (£50/$85). Plates: H.M. Stanley, 10" diam. (£40/ $70) and Glasgow International Exhibition of 1888, 10"diam. (£80/$135).

6.24. Plates: Tonkin, 9.75" diam. (£35/$60). Mask pitchers, 7.25" and 8" ht.(£40/$70).

6.25. Plate: Cable, 10.25" diam.(£30/$50). Pitchers with pink ground, 6" ht. (£50/$85).

6.26. A different "Stanley" plate, 9.75" diam. (£45/$75).

6.27. Various late shapes and patterns. Serving dish (£45/$75); teapot (£60/$100); red pitcher (£60/$100); moulded pitcher (£35/60).

7

Bridgeness Pottery, Bo'ness

Charles W. McNay, founder of the Bridgeness Pottery, was a Glaswegian by birth but had spent much of his life in Bo'ness where he had risen to be manager of the Bo'ness Pottery. By the 1880s this had fallen on hard times and in 1886 C.W. McNay founded the nearby Bridgeness Pottery, though production did not start before 1888. The pottery had 5 kilns and the latest in machinery and employed 200 workers. Charles' brother George was manager.

The pottery was immediately successful. Much material was said to have been bought from the Bo'ness Pottery on its closure and Bridgeness to have fallen heir to many of its customers. Charles died in 1913, leaving the pottery to his three sons, though only Josiah and Charles took an active role in running the works. Josiah died in 1941 leaving Charles as sole owner. Under his management the pottery slowly declined, finally closing in 1959.

On opening, the pottery made the usual domestic transfer-printed white earthenware. The body was rather coarse but many of the patterns, such as Burns (7.1), Delph (7.4) and Forth Bridge (7.2) were very popular locally. Burns is frequently marked Carron due to confusion with a very similar, though less popular pattern. Patterns carried over from Bo'ness Pottery include Bosphorus (7.4) and that universal favourite Grecian, made by so many potteries all over Britain as both a transfer and a sponge print. Both these patterns were re-engraved by the Bridgeness Works. Throughout its life the pottery produced much spongeware, though it was seldom marked. A catalogue printed for the Irish market is known. At some point in its life the Bridgeness Pottery made stoneware but so far only one piece has been recognised — a hot water bottle.

After World War One slip casting was introduced and, gradually, other decorative innovations. Stenciled patterns were printed in outline and clobbered carefully. During the Second World War, of course, only plain white ware (7.8) or simple blue-banded ware could be made and even for some years thereafter. On an order, for instance, for the Corporation of Glasgow, the pottery was able to decorate only with a tiny coat of arms in black outline (7.8). During the War, and especially afterwards, gummed paper labels were much used as marks and, as these have mostly gone, it can be difficult to identify such wares.

When Government restrictions were lifted the Bridgeness Pottery reacted immediately. They had employed a mould maker named Horace Elsmore who had come to Bo'ness in 1947 from North Staffordshire. During the early 1950s, Elsmore produced a series of very modern shapes and patterns, using very bright colours and spray-painting on vases, jugs and plates. These were given names such as Royal, Celtic and Aintree and were quite successful with the public.

Pottery Descriptions: C.W. McNay — printed
C.W. McNay & Sons — printed

Reading: Roberts, Christine and Lyon, Beverly. 'Bo'ness Potteries' — Falkirk Museum (1977)

Pattern List:

Aberdeen — known from sherd.
Aintree — spray of flowers.
Autumn — a pheasant and a fox.
Bosphorus
Broseley — the usual variant of Willow.
Burns
Caledonia — landscapes (not all Scottish!).
Carron
Celtic
Circus — a circus scene for Christmas.
Commerce — an allegorical figure.
Dado
Delph
Erin
Fan
Fearns — grasses and ferns.
Fiji
Forth Bridge
Glasgow International Exhibition 1888
Grange
Grecian — the usual pattern.
Mavis — bird on twig.
Paragon
Royal

Rustic — a 'Japanese' pattern.
Spray
Summer
Teck
York — a 'Japanese' pattern.

7.1. Wall plaques with Burns, a pattern used also for porringers, punch bowls and cream and sugar sets. It is often found marked Carron but this name seems more correctly to belong to a rarer pattern with a central domestic scene — 9.5" diam. (£70/$120)

7.2. Wall plaques with Forth Bridge, 9.5" diam. (£40/$70) and Glasgow International Exhibition 1888, 10" diam. (£80/$135). Bowl with latter pattern, 5.5" diam. (£60/$100).

7.3. Wall plaque, 9.5" diam. (£50/$85) and pitcher, 8.5" ht. (£70/$120) with Christmas scene.

7.4. Plates: Delph, 8" diam. (£20/$35) and Bosphorus (£20/$35). Bowl: Fiji, 5.5" diam. (£35/$60).

7.5. Mark on Delph plate.

7.6. Bowl with Christmas scene, 5.5" diam. (£50/$85). Plates: Paragon, 9" diam. (£15/$25) and Summer, 9" diam. (£25/$40). Sauceboat: Fiji (£20/$35).

7.7. Bowls for Christmas and Queen Victoria's jubilee, 5.5" diam. (£45, 50/$75, 85).

7.8. Wartime wares. Large pitcher, 8" ht. (£25/$40). Small pitcher, 5.75" ht. (£15/$25). Daisy plate, 7" diam. (£5/$8). Bowl, 5" diam. (£15/$25).

7.9. Cup, saucer and teaplate said to have been decorated at the Bridgeness Pottery but unmarked (£35/$60).

7.10. Mug: sponge-printed with cows on grass, unmarked but certainly made by McNay's, 4" ht. (£70/$120).

8

Britannia Pottery, Glasgow

In the 1840s Robert Cochran got control of the Verreville Pottery and transformed it into a commercial success. But by the time he had done this he had set his sights on the export trade. Verreville, being of old design, was quite unsuitable for mechanisation and there was no room for expansion. So Cochran, still in partnership with his brother Alexander, bought land next to their glass works and erected a new pottery in the 1850s in the north quarter of Glasgow and called it the Britannia Pottery.

This was a 12-kiln pottery, fully mechanised for its period and built specifically to supply the North American market, since Cochran already had a depot in Canada. During its first years of life, the Pottery produced solely white ironstone in huge quantities which is found much more frequently in the USA and Canada than in Britain. This is true of all white ironstone produced in Britain. Decoration was purely in the moulding with wheat ears or beavers, etc., or else in pink lustre sometimes over underglaze blue or with green. From 1857 until c.1863 this was the only known product, but after that transfer-printed wares began to appear on the home market and Britannia traded successfully on both sides of the Atlantic.

Robert Cochran died on 7 August 1869 but by then he had made provision for his oldest son, Alexander, to take over the pottery in partnership with the manager, James Fleming. These two ran the pottery throughout the rest of the century — taking Fleming's son, Arnold, as partner in 1896. Eventually Cochran died and James Fleming retired in 1911, leaving Arnold in sole charge. In 1920 he sold the pottery to a consortium of businessmen who traded as Britannia Pottery Co. Ltd. until 1939.

At no time did Britannia make china. White earthenware was its sole product, except for an experiment in the early 20th century with agate ware. Decoration was mainly by transfer-print but hand-painting, sponge-printing and mocha were practised. In the later years of the 19th century, a heavy ware was made for shipping and Cochran's 2 lb. white jam jars were a celebrated innovation in their day. The Pottery was designed purely as a business proposition to make the wares that Cochran knew he could sell. A series of Christmas jugs was produced in the 1880s, rivaled only by those of Clyde Pottery. A few large, elaborately-painted vases are known. A series of views of Quebec was produced for a dealer, M. Thomas, in that city; production continued into the last period of the pottery's life. The edging for the pieces showed maple leaves and beavers. Britannia also had a firm foothold in the south-east Asian market with their special designs, largely founded upon Bells' originals. Spongeware was made throughout.

In the 'Limited' period the wares were changed completely. Jazz designs and bright colours were used on a 'Scotch Ivory' body invented by Arnold Fleming but developed under the later owners. The wares of this period are still found abundantly. A series of oriental scenes in coloured transfer known as 'Omar Khayyam' was particularly popular. Spongeware was also produced as well as simpler wares for the ordinary dinner table.

Little of the white ironstone that Cochran made for the American market has remained in Scotland but even the little that we have seems to be more than survived from English potteries in England, although they made many times more. What does remain seems very similar to that made in Staffordshire. The Ceres pattern (8.1), of which variants were made by so many potteries, survives in Cochran's version on both sides of the Atlantic as do the teapots with moulded beavers on both sides and the lid, made for Canada. Pieces decorated with a simple gold line or two and a gold 'shamrock' were also popular and were made over a long period. As well as these, transfer printed pitchers to celebrate the 1863 wedding of the Prince of Wales to Princess Alexandra and the 1871 wedding of the Marquis of Lorne to Princess Louise were made. The latter proved very popular in Canada where the Marquis was Governor-General for many years. In North America only variants of white ironstone have been found decorated with crimson and green enamel or pink lustre over blue. Marks on all of these are very varied (8.2-4).

It should be noted that some confusion may arise here since both Britannia and Verreville referred to themselves as R.Cochran & Co. at this time and at a later period again. In fact they also often shared transfer patterns while Robert Cochran senior was alive. The addition of St. Rollox to the pottery description places the piece firmly as being Britannia's.

Once the pottery began to sell its wares in Britain, we have a great preponderance of transfer-printing, which in the 1860s and 1870s was the dominant form of decoration, whether in purple, blue, brown, black, green or even flow blue. Patterns were very varied. India shows a rich scene of empire, China reflects trade interests and has even been found in Java, Wide Awake is for the more sentimentally inclined (8.5). Duchess was a particularly favoured pattern used for wall plaques as well as pitchers and continued for a long time until the copper plate had totally degenerated into almost indecipherable blobs (8.7). The pottery description settles for a time as COCHRAN. Other patterns on pitchers include Fern and Stag as well as unmarked moulded pitchers with Burns' head. One pitcher in this shape shows vignettes of two of the four seasons and must have been one of a pair. The other two seasons have been recorded on a jug of slightly later shape (8.10).

Other pieces known with the same mark as Duchess are Chrysanthemum, found on dinner ware and bedroom sets in olive, Persia and Pimflowe(r). The former is a 'Japanese' pattern of the sort which became the craze in the 1870s, the latter shows the influence of the Arts and Crafts Movement (8.11). Greek appears on two pitcher shapes in two different colors. Fruit was made in several colors and often clobbered (8.12, 18). The pottery description had now at least partially reverted to R.COCHRAN & Co. Rose appeared only on bowls but Rose Wreath (8.13) and Rose and Lily were popular, the latter also on punch bowls (8.15, 39). Dancing Cupids, Summer pattern and Vase all appear on pitchers (8.15, 16). As well as this, we have unmarked pitchers showing scenes of Edinburgh and others in jet, reminding us that Britannia made colored wares, spongeware and commercial slipwares, none of which would be marked (8.14). One jelly mould has been recorded in pure white (8.13).

The straight-sided pitcher which had the seasons prints was a great success and appeared in many guises including one for a Glasgow Exhibition (8.16). Other patterns include Spring, Auld Acquaintance (8.19), Good Cheer and Christmas and other Christmas patterns of which this Pottery produced a good number (8.20). The heyday of this pitcher shape was the 1880s. Dinner services seem to have been neglected all through this period though Wild Rose is known (8.21). The export trade on the other hand was anything but neglected. All through Britannia's life, even during its final period, it exported in some quantity to Canada. A set of views of Quebec was made for a dealer, M.C.Thomas. These are widely distributed in Canada but rare in Britain though sherds have been found in Britannia dumps (see later). Spongeware must also have been sent over the Atlantic but, being unmarked, has remained unknown. The only exception to this is the well known spongeware pattern Grecian of which some very degenerate examples are found with a Cochran mark (8.29). Something more is known of the export trade to South East Asia for which plates seem to have been modeled on the export transfer designs of Bells. Canton, Colombo (8.21) and Agra (8.42) are amongst the patterns known.

At this time too, until the advent of the Limited Company, the pottery descriptions become completely useless chronologically. R.COCHRAN & Co., COCHRAN & Co., COCHRAN & FLEMING, C. & F. and FLEMING seem to be used with careless abandon, sometimes in combination.

Octagonal plates were produced as wall plaques, souvenirs of Glasgow or Edinburgh, and some with Jubilee (8.22). A number of unmarked pitchers were made, mostly hexagonal with little coloured roses and fairly crude hand painting (8.23). Meanwhile, hotel wares and wares for shipping, potted very thickly, were made in large quantity but have scarcely survived (8.40, 41).

Towards the end of the nineteenth century, under the influence of J. Arnold Fleming and of fashion, the wares changed considerably in character. At this time, or slightly earlier, a number of fairly ambitious hand-painted vases were manufactured (8.43-45) but, judging by their rarity, they seem not to have sold well. Wall plaques and other pieces painted in blue and white with Dutch scenes seem to have been more successful (8.46), as were others with floral designs (8.30). Souvenirs for the Glasgow Exhibition of 1901 are still very plentiful (8.26-28). A very large cup and saucer made for this occasion was revived for the East End Exhibition of 1903 and generally (8.30, 37). An old Verreville pattern, Syria, was also reproduced, sometimes heavily decorated (8.34 & 8.38).

But the main innovation was to make rather wispy floral edge designs, often clobbered in pale colors, or else to color designs very heavily (8.30, 32, 34, 36, 37, 38). This is particularly true of dinner services which were made in large quantities at this time. One interesting plate, printed in pale green, seems to have been made for a special occasion which has not been identified (8.37). It shows a yacht on a river (almost certainly the Clyde) with a paddle steamer approaching from the right. Agate ware was made in four colors of clay: white, light blue, dark blue and brown (8.36). An oval pitcher shape was produced in large numbers at this time and used in commemoratives (8.26, 32) for exhibitions, Queen Victoria's death, and George V's Coronation, and is known with Tulip which also appears on other pitchers (8.34) and on teapots.

It is clear that every opportunity to make a salable article was being eagerly grasped in the face of many difficulties but by 1923 Fleming decided to retire and sold the pottery to a group of Glasgow businessmen. It is impossible not to think of the last period of Britannia Pottery, when it was known as Britannia Pottery Co. Ltd., as a completely separate entity. Fleming had allowed the products to become completely old fashioned and divorced from contemporary taste. The new owners modernised shapes and patterns totally with the exception of the body of the wares. Fleming had been experimenting with a slightly yellowed body which would not clash with the bright colours coming into favour. The new Company turned production entirely over to this and called it Scotch Ivory, incorporating this name sometimes into their mark (8.47).

Very little else was retained from the old wares but one or two patterns were made which appealed to older taste (8.46). Very few patterns were given a name but many had a four-digit number, frequently painted on the back of the piece (8.47). Ming was among the few named patterns (8.48). Large numbers of dinner services and fruit sets were produced with minimal decoration round the rim either in colored transfer or painted (8.49-52). These were meant for the bottom end of the market.

The real attempt to become leaders in their field, and a unique attempt in Scottish pottery to keep up with contemporary taste, was in their more highly decorated wares. These frequently attained a depth of color by no means common in ceramics of the time.

Lanark Ware was Britannia's attempt to modernise Wemyss Ware's type of decoration since the original, made in Kirkcaldy, was by now on its last legs (8.53). Lanark Ware mostly consists of groups of fruit outlined in black with a green border, though occasional pieces with chickens are found. They are hand-painted and this became a much more common method of decoration at this time (8.54). An intense yellow was used on many wares, sometimes combined with black (8.55, 56). A very deep blue was developed and used with green and gold to paint large flowers on a bright orange background of thickly applied enamel (8.57) or on a pink ground spattered with purple (8.58). This ground also appeared with fruit (8.69).The deep blue (8.60) was used to great effect in a series of patterns known collectively as Omar Khayyam (8.61-68). There are eight known major scenes in the series though sometimes fresh scenes are made up with fragments of colored transfer from the major ones. The series was immensely successful, even promotional figures have been recorded, made for the stores that sold the ware. The sky is normally shown in intense blue but specimens are known with pink skies or violet or with opalescent glaze or an orange border instead (8.67, 68).

Ginger jars and sandwich plates (8.70) were made in some quantity. Nostalgic scenes from the past and boldly colored stripes were new forms of decoration. Flowers painted in bright colors, sometimes rather crudely, were very popular (8.71, 72, 76.) as were jazzy patterns and colored transfers of food (8.73).

Wares made for one of the partners and his wife's personal use had the mark SOLFRED painted on the bottom with a date (8.74, 75). Transfer printed patterns were made, one of which — Moyen — was shared with other potteries (8.77- 79). As well as the highly colored products, some were produced simply glazed and otherwise undecorated (8.80, 81). Marks throughout the period varied in detail but almost all showed Britannia, though the place of manufacture varies from Glasgow through Scotland to Great Britain (8.83). Spongeware was also made (8.82).

For some time at least the pottery continued to supply M.C.Thomas of Quebec with his souvenir wares (8.84) and in 1931 they produced a set of tea ware for a children's club run by a Glasgow newspaper. These pieces showed characters from a strip cartoon and had their own mark (8.84, 85). The Works is known to have employed art students during the summer months as painters and there are certainly some elaborately painted plaques and other pieces to be found (8.84). The Company made huge efforts to keep up with public taste but the struggle was relentless and with the outbreak of war in 1939 the owners decided to give up and close the pottery down. No trace is now left of it.

Pottery Descriptions: all printed

COCHRAN
R. COCHRAN & Co.
COCHRAN & FLEMING or C. & F.
also the above with ENGLAND
FLEMING — also impressed
B.P.Co.Ltd.
BRITANNIA POTTERY Co. Ltd.

Reading: Coutts, Howard "Four Plate Designs By Mackintosh" in *SPHR* 13 (1989): 74-77.

Fleming, J.A. *Scottish Pottery* is particularly relevant because Fleming was for a time the owner.

Kelly H.E. "The Life of Robert Cochran of Britannia and Verreville Potteries" in *Scottish Industrial History* 18 (1996): 8-20.

— "Robert Cochran's Potteries, White Ironstone and Tea Leaf Ware" in *Tea Leaf Readings* Vol. 17 Issue 3 — USA July 1997: 10-11.

Pattern List:

Agra
Ailsa — group of flowers against grating
Argyle — bird clinging to water plant
Auld Acquaintance
Bee and Rose — an export pattern
Ceylon
China
China Dragon — an export pattern featuring a dragon
Christmas
Chrysanthemum
Clyde — floral, against a tinted background
Colombo
Cyprus pattern — a "Japanese" pattern
Dancing Cupids
Diana — floral
Delft — a stylised vase
Duchess
Etruscan Shield — an export pattern
Fruit
Glasgow International Exhibition 1901
Good Cheer
Grecian
Greek
Holly
Humming Bird and Rose — an export pattern
India
In Memoriam
Japan — an export pattern
Jubilee
Korti — a "Japanese" pattern
Lily — a "Japanese" pattern
Louise
Mallow — mallow flowers
Mayflower — floral
Mona — Celtic interlace border
Moselle — border of poppies
Mungo — an export pattern with overall flowers and 'crackled' background.
Pansy — pansies.
Paris — floral border.
Pekin — oriental scene.
Persia
Petunia — petunias.
Pimflowe(r)
Pomegranate — an export pattern.
Poppy
Rose
Rose and Lily
Rose Wreath
Rowena
Shanghai — an export pattern
Sir Garnet Wolsely — bust of man
Sons of the Empire — soldiers
Spring
Stag
Summer pattern
Sunflower
Swiss Scenery
Syria
Tulip
Vase — two different patterns
Wide Awake
Wild Flower pattern
Wild Rose — the usual
Willow — the usual
Willow Victoria — Willow with a different border

Very few patterns are known from the last period. Amongst them are: *Delft, Moyen, Palermo, Pheasant, Rural England, San Toi, Wild Rose, and Willow*

8.1. Export wares: white ironstone sugar bowls (£20, 40/$35, 65) and royal wedding pitcher, 8" ht. (£90/$150) — teapot with moulded beavers, 9.5" ht.(£100/$170).

8.2-4. Marks from export wares portrayed in 8.1.

8.6. Mark.

8.5. Pitchers: India, Wide Awake, China, approx. 8" ht. (£90/$150 each).

8.8. Mark.

8.7. Duchess, showing decay of pattern. Wall plaques, 10.5" diam. (£120/$200) and pitchers, 8" ht. (£40-80/$65-135).

8.9. Pitchers: Stag, Fern and Burns' commemorative, 8" ht. (£40-50/ $65-85).

8.10. Porringer: Rose, 6.75" diam. (£35/$60). Pitchers with 'The Seasons', 8" ht. (£90/$150).

8.11. Ashet, 11" lgth. (£25/$40) and porringer, 6" diam. (£35/$60): Persia. Porringer: Pimflowe(r.) [imperfect mark], 6.25" diam. (£35/$60). Ewer, 10.5" ht. (£100/170): Sunflower.

8.12. Pitchers: Fruit, Greek, Holly - 8" ht. (£30-60/$50-100 each).

8.13. Jelly mould and pitchers: Rose Wreath, 8" ht. (£40/$70).

8.14. Unmarked pitchers, approx. 8" ht. (£40-90/$70-150 each).

8.15. Pitchers: Rose and Lily, Dancing Cupids, Christmas and Summer pattern [so named], approx. 7.75" ht. (£40-90/$70-150).

8.16. Pitchers: Vase, 8" ht. (£40/$70) and a commemorative for a Glasgow Exhibition (£90/150).

8.17, 18. Marks.

8.19. Pitchers: Auld Acquaintance, Spring, 8" ht. (£90/$150).

8.20. Christmas pitchers: Good Cheer, unnamed, Christmas [at back] and unnamed, 8" ht. (£90-120/$150-200).

8.21. Export plate: Canton, 9.5" diam. (£65/$110). Rice dish: Colombo, approx. 9.5" diam. (£65/$110). Plate: Wild Rose, approx. 9.5" diam. (£50/$85). Unnamed large cup and saucer attributed to Britannia (cup is 5.25" diam.) (£35/$60).

8.22. Octagonal plates: souvenir of Glasgow and of Edinburgh with Jubilee between, 9.75" diam. (£55/$90).

8.23. Unmarked pitchers, approx. 8" ht. (£30-40/$50-70).

8.24, 25. Marks.

8.26. Exhibition of 1901 in Glasgow: souvenir wares — pitcher, 8.5" ht. (90/$150), biscuit barrel, approx. 6" ht. (£50/$65), large cup and saucer [cup is 5.25" diam.] (£100/$170), plates, 9-9.5" diam. (£50/$85) and bonbon dishes, approx. 3" diam. (£15/$25).

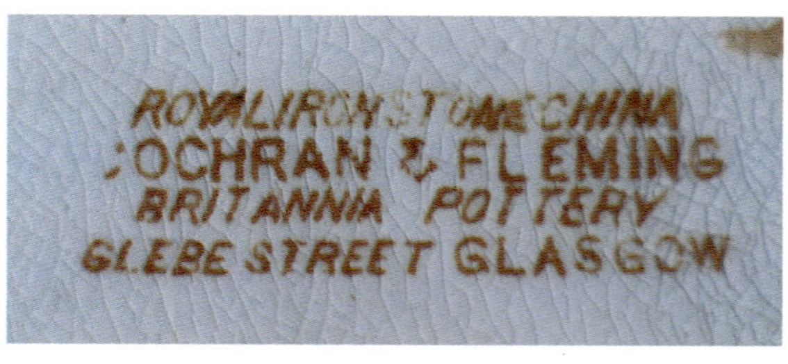

8.27. Mark on the wares seen in 8.26.

8.28. Souvenir of 1901 Exhibition, bowl, approx. 6" ht. (£40/$70). Pitchers: Poppy, approx. 6.5" ht. (£35/$60) and unnamed (£35/$60). Patriotic plate, 8.5" diam. (£50/$85) and unnamed plate, approx. 8.5" (£15/$25).

8.29. Ashet: Grecian in a very degenerate state (£50/$85).

8.30. Large cup and saucer, 5.25" diam. (£60/$100), wall plaque (£60/$100) and unnamed sauceboat (£10/$15) and plate (£15/$25).

8.31. Mark.

8.33. Mark.

Above: 8.32. Pitchers: for 1911 Coronation of George V and Queen Mary, 8.75" ht. (£90/$150) and for Queen Victoria's death in 1901, approx. 6.5" ht.(£50/$85), Rowena, 8.75" ht. (£40/$70) [with plate, 9" diam. (£10/$15)] and unnamed (£30/$50).

Below: 8.34. Pitcher: Tulip, 7.75" ht. (£35/$60). Plates: Louise, unnamed, Syria — all approx. 9" diam. (£10-15/$15-25).

8.35. Mark.

8.36. Agate ware vases, 4.5" ht. (£60/$100). Plate: Strawberry, 8.5" diam. (£25/$40). Vase: imitation of Wemyss Ware's Turkish pattern, 4.75" ht. (£40/$70).

8.37. Yachting plate, 8.5" diam. (£45/$75), large cup, 5.25" diam. (£10-15/$17-25). Plate: Chrysanthemum, approx. 9" diam. Plate (approx. 9") and ashet (approx. 11"): Wild Flower pattern. Last three (£10-15/$17-25).

8.38. Plate: Syria in red with deep blue clobbering, approx. 8.5" diam. (£15/$25).

8.39. Punch bowl: Rose and Lily, 9.75" diam. (£65/$110).

8.40. Plate: hotel ware [damaged], approx. 6" diam. (£5/$13).

8.41. Plate: ship's ware - J.& G.T. Ltd., approx. 7.75" diam. (£15/$25).

8.42. Export plate: Agra, approx. 8" diam. (£30/$50).

8.43, 44, 45. Painted vases (£200/$340).

8.47. Mark.

8.46. Plates: back row Peony and unnamed, approx. 8" diam. (£10/$15 each); front row: unnamed (same).

8.48. Ming plates and unnamed pattern with heron. B.P.Co. Ltd. Plates, 9" diam. (£10/$15). Octagonal plates, approx. 8" diam. (£20/$35). Vase, approx. 7" ht. (£25/$40).

8.49, 50, 51, 52. Edge patterns from B.P.Co. Ltd. - no name - front centre Palermo - dinner sets, fruit sets, tea sets, etc. Bread plate, 9.75" bdth. (£30/$50) and pitcher, 6" ht. (£30/$50) with rose and deep blue background. The rest (£10/$15 each).

8.53. Lanark ware. Large plate, 11.5" diam.(£90/$150). Bowl, 10" diam. (£60/$100). Plate, 7.25" diam. (£20/$35). Cup & saucer, 6" diam. (£30/$50). Shallow bowl, 8.5" diam. (30/$50).

8.54. Mark.

8.55. Yellow and yellow and black decorated tea ware and egg cups. Tea plate, 7" diam. (£25/$40 with cup and saucer). Egg cups, 6" lgth. (£ 25/$40). Striped saucers, 5" diam. (£2/$3).

8.56. Back: plate with San Toi, 8.25" diam. (£20/$35), vase, 4.5" ht. (£35/$60). Front: unnamed, 9" lgth. and 7" diam. (£10/$15 each).

8.57. Wares with blue flower and orange enamel. Small vases, 3.5" ht. (£20/$35). Serving dish, 9.5" diam. (£25/$40). Bowl, 8.25" diam. (£40/$70). Deep plate, 7.25" diam. (£20/$35).

8.58. Blue flowers with pink and purple. Vase, 4.5" ht. (£35/$60). Bonbonniere, 7.25" lgth. (£20/$35) — other colored wares: small vases, 4.5" ht. (£25/$40 each). Bowl, 9" diam. (£30/$50).

8.59. Wares with dragonfly pattern. Bowl, 9" diam. (£50/$85). Small bowl, 8" diam. (£30/$50). Vase, 8" ht. (£30/$50). Plate, 5" diam., small vase, 3.5" ht. (£20/$35 each).

8.60. Colored wares. Biscuit Barrel, 6.5" ht.(£40/$70). Bowl, 9" diam. (£30/$50). Plate, approx. 6" diam. (£10/$17).

8.61. Omar Khayyam: The Snake Charmer. Vase, 11.5" ht. (with lid £90/$150). Ginger jar, 9.75" ht.(£90/$150). Plate, 9" diam. (£70/120).

8.62. Omar Khayyam: The Story Teller. Plate, 9" diam. (£70/$120). Bowl, 7" diam. (£30/$50). Jar, approx. 5" ht. (£25/$40).

8.63. Omar Khayyam: The Potter. Large vase, approx. 8" ht. (£35/$60). Small vase, 5.25" ht. (£35/$60). Bowl, approx. 7" diam. (£35/$60). Ginger jar, 4.5" ht. (£40/$70 with lid).

8.64. Omar Khayyam: The Merchant: plate, 9" diam. (£70/$120) and The Caravan Passing: plate, 9" diam. (£70/$120), biscuit barrel, 5.75" ht. (£50/$85).

8.65. Omar Khayyam: Camels passing left to right: plate, 9" diam. (£50/$85), pitcher, 5.75" ht.(£50/$85) and market scene: coffee cup & saucer, 4" diam. (£40/$70).

8.66. Omar Khayyam: Men outside the town. Sandwich plate, approx. 15" (£100/$170), plate, 9" (£60/$100), bowl, 8" diam. (£35-$60).

8.67. Omar Khayyam: variants with violet sky or orange stripes. Plates, 9" diam. (£50/$85). Ginger jar, 5.5" ht. (£50/$85). Vase, 3.5" ht. (£35/$60).

8.68. Omar Khayyam: variants with pink sky or opalescent glaze. Plates, 10" diam. (£50/$85) each. Small ginger jar, 5.5" ht. (£50/$85 with lid). Opalescent glazed jar, 6.5" ht. (£60/$100 with or without lid).

8.69, 70. Colored and edge wares. Sandwich plates, 11.75" lgth. (£10, 25/$17, 40). Ginger jar, 9.75" ht. (£40/$70 without lid). Octagonal plate, 8" diam. (£40/$70). Others (£10-20/$17-35).

8.71. Painted flowers. Sandwich plate, 11.75" lgth. (£30/$50). Vase, 7.5" ht. (£30/$50). Pitcher, 6.75" ht. (£25/$40). Plates, 8.5" diam. (£10-$17).

8.72. Painted flowers and stamped cherries. Chamber pot, 9.25" diam. (£30$50). Vases, 5.5" ht.(£20/$35). Pitcher, 5" ht. (£25/$40).

8.73. Jazzy and food patterns. Plates, 7.75" - 9" diam. (£35/$60 each).

8.74. Tea and coffee wares. Teapot, 8.25" lgth, coffee pot, 6.75" ht. (£30/$50 each). Cookie barrel, 6.75" ht. (£25/$40). Water pitcher, 6.5" ht. (£20/$35).

8.75. SOLFRED mark.

8.76. Painted flowers. Serving dish, 9.5" diam. (£30/$50). Sauceboat, 6" lgth. (£10/$17). Plate, 9.5" diam. (£10/$17). Pitcher, 5" (£25/$40).

8.77. Moyen pattern. Plates, 8.75" diam. (£10-15/ $17-25).

8.78. Mark for Moyen pattern plate seen in 8.77.

8.79. Plates: back: unnamed and Pheasant; front: Rural England and Delft. All 8.75" diam. (£10-20/$17-25)

8.80. White wares and biscuit barrel. Vase, 10" ht. (£30/$50). Teapot, 7" lgth. (£20/$35). Cookie barrel, 6.5" ht. (£40/$70).

8.81. White ware and colored transfers. Platter, 12.25" lgth. (£20/$35). Pitcher (£20/$35). Sauceboat, 6" lgth. (£10/$17).

8.82. Bowl: sponge printed in pink and olive, 6.75" diam. (£50/$85)

8.83. Mark.

8.84. Back: Quebec view for M.C. Thomas, 11.25" diam. (£100/$170). Front: Chum Club plate, 6.5" diam. (£25/$40) and wall plaque, 12.25" lgth. (£85/$100).

8.85. Chums Club mark.

8.86. Painted 'Dutch' plaque (£200/$340).

8.87. Export Plate returned from Sri Lanka, approx. 11" diam. (£100/$120).

9 A.W. Buchan & Co. Ld. — Portobello and Crieff

There were at least two potteries in Portobello, east of Edinburgh, in the late eighteenth and the early nineteenth centuries. This one was known at various times as the Bridge St. or Waverley Pottery. Its early history seems not to be very clearly known. In fact it seems not always to have been a pottery but to have had a period as a soap works.

The first owners to emerge with any certainty as potters from the cloud of ignorance are Milne, Cornwall & Co. The 'Co.' seems to have included a Hugh Smith but, apart from names, little is known of the partners. They occupied the premises as a stoneware pottery from the early 1830s but were gone before the 1851 Census.

The next owners were T. & R. Tough, who quickly became T.Tough & Co.; they worked the pottery certainly until 1867. In that or the following year the firm became Murray and Buchan. Alexander Willison Buchan was a farmer's son who worked as a 'traveler' (salesman) for a whisky firm. Why he decided to enter the world of pottery-making is not known but he prudently formed a partnership of association with Thomas F. Murray. Murray was a member of the family which ran the very successful Caledonian Pottery in Glasgow who made, amongst other bodies, stoneware of very high quality. Murray's function was obviously to teach A.W. Buchan the business.

Over the year Buchan bought Murray out until, by 1882, the firm was known as A.W. Buchan & Co. Buchan's sons entered the business as they became old enough and the pottery has remained in the family's hands until this time. In 1972, in search of more space and a government grant, the works was moved to Crieff in Perthshire although, confusingly, pieces are still marked 'Portobello'.

The wares of the Milne, Cornwall & Co. period are little known apart from a large saltglazed stoneware water filter in the Royal Museum, but sherd evidence reveals that the usual run of stoneware goods was made. They have been credited in the literature in the past with some elaborate salt buckets with 'Tam O'Shanter' among other figures; however, these are now known to have been made at the Caledonian Pottery in Glasgow. Tough & Co. are said to have made only redware, none of which has been identified. Murray & Buchan reverted to stoneware production and storage jars, whisky jars and ginger beer bottles are prominent among the products known.

Under Buchan himself, the usual run of stoneware goods was produced, including drinking fonts and hot water bottles. Towards the end of the nineteenth century, the pottery produced Portobello Faience, wares in a colored stoneware body decorated with coloured slips. In the 1920s they started a line in spiked vases and square flower vases for use in graveyards, known respectively as Portovase and Senolith (9.9). From 1945 painted and printed wares were made, often on a light blue base, many with painted thistles (9.4-8). Many of the wares are now slip cast.

Pottery Descriptions: H.Cornwall potter — impressed

Murray & Buchan — impressed

Buchan — printed, stamped or impressed

A.W. Buchan & Co. — impressed

Portovase — stamped.

Reading: Hill, Robin A. *A History of A.W.Buchan & Co. Ltd.* (2nd edition — Edinburgh 1997) — this is the classic text.

Cruickshank, G. "Portobello Saltglaze" in *SPHR* 6 (1981): 42-43.

— "Waverley Potteries" and "Portobello Saltglaze" — both in *SPHR* 7 (1982): 15-23.

— "Buchan's Pottery, Portobello — the final days" in *A Sense of Place* (Edinburgh 1988): 37-50.

9.1. Lidded butter dish (£45/$75) and whisky barrel (£80/$135).

9.2. Three butter dishes with retailer's names and addresses (£45-60/$75-100 each).

9.3. Whisky flagon (£50/$85).

9.4. Self-colored and souvenir wares, creamers, ash trays, pitcher and bowl (£15-20/$25-35 each).

9.5. Painted wares (£20-30/$35-50 each).

9.6. Painted wares with (back) a coal-fired vase (£30-40/$50-70 each).

9.7. Painted lidded jar (£30/$50) and Thistle Ware bowl (£20/$35).

9.8. Thistle ware. Teapot, 9.75" long (£30/$50), bowls, 5.75" diam. (£10/$17), and mug, 4.75" ht. (£15/$25).

9.9. Painted and printed wares — two Portovases, 9" ht. (£25/$40 each), one mug to commemorate a royal visit to John Brown's Shipyard in Clydebank in 1986, 3.25" ht. (£25/$40), smaller pieces (£10/$17).

10

Caledonian Pottery, Glasgow

This Pottery was founded in 1800 near the Forth & Clyde Canal in the northern part of the city of Glasgow. The founding firm consisted of a group of Glasgow merchants trading as Reid, Paterson & Co. Robert Reid under the pseudonym Senex later wrote a valuable series of articles on Glasgow in the eighteenth century reprinted in *Glasgow Past and Present*.

It was a very ambitious Pottery, making from the start porcelain, creamware, coloured wares, redware and bricks as well as stoneware. Potters were imported from Staffordshire. The Pottery was known by several names initially, including Glasgow Pottery and Townhead Pottery but after a few years settled into Caledonian Pottery.

In 1810 the pottery was experiencing difficulties and was bought by the Delftfield Co. whose Pottery on the banks of the river Clyde was very confined by other works. They moved in during the next year and adopted the name Caledonian so the Delftfield Company ceased to exist as such. However, in 1823 the pottery was again for sale and bought by John Kemp & Co. who lasted only until 1826.

In that year William Murray and his sons Alexander and William junior purchased the pottery as Murray & Co. The works was known as Caledonian Pottery and Townhead Grinding Works. It is possible that at this time of economic depression firebricks and drainpipes were made from fire clay but certainly white earthenware and coloured wares were also made. The Murrays were enlightened employers who founded a Scientific Institution for their workers with a lending library and winter lecture courses. Workers were summoned in the mornings by a clerk blowing on a cow horn which must have delighted others living in the area.

In 1835 a clay tobacco pipe works was erected next door which was the especial province of William senior, who continued to run it even after he retired from the main business, which he did in 1840. William Murray junior took as partners James Couper and John Fullarton. The latter was his brother-in-law. James Couper had had previous experience in making both ceramics and glass in partnership with Robert Cochran. He went on to greater fame as the maker of Clutha Glass. He left the partnership in 1850 after which the firm became Murray & Fullarton.

About 1860 William Murray junior's eldest son, Wm. Fullarton Murray, was old enough to join the Pottery as a partner. On the death of William senior in 1862 the pipe works was sold off. Then in 1864 the texts say that both Wm. Murray jun. and J. Fullarton retired, leaving Wm. F. Murray in charge in partnership with Frederick Grosvenor but since pieces of this period are marked Murrays & Grosvenor we must assume either that Wm. junior was still working or that another member of the family was involved. Grosvenor was an English businessman, born in Staffordshire, who had ambitions to run a stoneware pottery and joined the partnership to learn the business. He left in 1868 to found the Eagle Pottery and Caledonian continued as Murray & Co. again.

For several years previously the pottery had had trouble with whitewares due to pollution from the neighbouring Glasgow Ironworks. In 1872 much of the pottery, perhaps all, was sold to the Iron-work Company and the business moved to new premises in Rutherglen, a small town to the east of Glasgow. Part of the old Pottery became the Crown Pottery, run by Miller & Young until the premises burnt down in 1879.

In 1895 John G. McIntyre, an Irish agent of the pottery, became a partner and the firm became W.F. Murray & Co. Ltd. In 1898 the Company went into sequestration but was bought immediately by W.P.Hartley of Liverpool, a jam manufacturer, in order to ensure a supply of stoneware jam jars. The advent of the glass jam jar put paid to the manufacture of the stoneware variety and in 1928 the pottery finally closed down.

This Pottery must be regarded as unique in Scotland for the variety of wares made by it through-out most of its life. It must be seen as a prolific maker of stoneware throughout (10.1-6). An early period of saltglaze was followed by Bristol or borax glazing but saltglaze was revived certainly during its time in Rutherglen. A series of saltglaze salt buckets decorated with elaborate, almost free-standing figures and multiple sprigs is well known from the 1850s. Usually they are brown with sprigs with the same iron wash but some are blue with white sprigs or vice-versa. One very large (56 cm. high) pitcher is known covered overall with different sprigs beautifully moulded. From the later period of Murray & Co. larger pieces of saltglaze are known. (10.5) Large and small barrels, round or oval, moulded to look like wooden staves are found with a Bristol glaze and saltglaze (10.3). Hot water bottles from Murray & Fullarton are known (10.1). Otherwise whisky flagons, cream jars, pie dishes, butter dishes and all the usual stoneware forms are common. Some unmarked figurines of a Glasgow beggar are attributed to the pottery.

Colored wares are quite frequently found. Black basalte tea services are well known with eagles perched on the handles of creams and teapots. They are never marked but are firmly attributed on sherd evidence (10.8). A few are found with copper lustre and hand-painting. Green dessert services are known with marks from Murray & Couper and the following periods (10.10). Blue jugs moulded with monkeys aping humans are attributed on J.A. Fleming's evidence. Splash-glazed dishes with multiple loop handles are also found. Mazarin blue was used for a short period (10.9).

Only one piece of marked porcelain is known but it has led to others. In transfer-printed ware the most popular pattern was The Chase in sepia found with Murray & Couper and Murray & Fullarton marks. This was a changing pattern used on dinner ware with very large platters (10.7). A pitcher was printed for the Great Exhibition of 1851 (10.7), otherwise the patterns tend to be very ordinary. One early group of plates is attributed to the pottery. They are printed in blue with a wide border of thistles, roses and shamrocks. The centre may show George III, Rabbie Burns, an early steamship or simply a basket of fruit. The attribution is attractive.

Less attractive is the attribution of a series of dishes printed in blue with a Spode pattern known to have been made also by other potteries. On the back is the printed legend ROWLEY.WILSON ST.GLASGOW.STONE CHINA Rowley had formerly been a manager of Caledonian and left to found a china warehouse. Opinions are divided about the origin of these pieces.

Pottery Descriptions: Townhead Pottery — incised
Caledonian — painted
Murray & Co. or M. & Co.— impressed
Murray & Couper or M. & C. — impressed or printed
Murray & Fullarton — impressed or printed
M. & F. — printed
Murray — impressed.

Reading: Fleming, J.A. "An Old Glasgow Industry" in *Transactions of the Old Glasgow Club* No.5 (1913): 310-314.
Neil, J.S. "The Story of the Caledonian Pottery" in *Transactions of the Old Glasgow Club* (1912)
Quail, G. *Caledonian Pottery* (Glasgow 1986) — this is the classic text

Pattern List:

All of the marked transfer patterns carry the pottery description M & C or M & F which restricts these patterns and perhaps the making of this sort of pottery to a very narrow band of time.

Affghan — a fantastic landscape
Balmoral — Castle with figures
Canton — oriental border
The Chase
Chinese
Convolvous — Convolvulus
Falconry
Lace
Moss Rose — same as the Bells' pattern
Passion Flower — sprig of flowers with central passion flower
Statue
Temple

10.1. Salt-glazed hot water bottle or foot warmer, 13" ht. (£40/$70) and large pickling (?) jar, 15" lgth. (£90/$150).

10.2. Mark on hot water bottle in 10.1.

10.4. Mark on large barrel above.

10.3. Round and oval whisky barrels, 8.75" and 16.25" ht. (£65/$110 each). Moulded pitcher, 7.5" ht. (£30/$50).

10.5. Large salt-glazed two-handled pitcher, 14.5" ht. (£90/$150). Storage jar (front), 8.5" ht. (£30/$50 with lid); storage jar (back), 8.5" ht. (£15/$25).

10.6. Moulded spittoon with Rockingham glaze, 9" diam. (£20/$35). Tobacco jar, approx. 6" ht. (£35/$ 60 with lid).

10.7. Plate: The Chase, 9.25" diam. (£35/$60). Pitcher for the Great Exhibition of 1851, 8" ht. (£75/$125).

10.8. Teapot, Sugar and creamer in black basalte (£120/$200 the set).

10.9. Two teapots decorated in mazarin blue, 8.25" and 9.5" ht. (£60, 70/$100, 120).

10.10. Two green dessert plates, 8.25" and 9.25" diam. (£35/$60 each).

10.11. Mark **editor there wasn't a caption for this slide**

11

Campbellfield Pottery, Glasgow

The life of this Pottery divides into two very different stages. In the first, it is situated in the Gallowgate in Glasgow's east end and is mainly a brick and tile work. In the second stage, it is situated in Springburn in the north of the City and is a whiteware pottery. Apart from the name, there is little connection between the two.

The Campbellfield estate was purchased in 1819 by William Wilson, a brickbuilder and owner of an inn, to be used as a brickwork. The entire area of Glasgow in which the estate was situated had a covering of clay which could be used to make bricks and other redware items, so the potteries of the area were digging their raw material out from under their works. Wilson's previous brickwork had been compulsorily purchased by Glasgow Town Council and he bought the estate to provide material for his building business. It was operated in a small way until 1827 when the pottery was expanded and functioned on a greater scale, still as a brick and tile work though some redware was probably made.

In 1849 William Wilson went bankrupt and various partnerships ran the works until Wilson's son, William junior, took over control in 1856. By this time the supply of clay from the Campbellfield estate was running out and the pottery becoming less profitable. In 1874 William junior sold out to a potter called William Rankine Currie who made redware on the site and Rockingham-glazed goods. It is possible that at this period he experimented with making whiteware.

In 1881 he formed a limited liability company with himself as principal shareholder. This Campbellfield Pottery Co. Ltd. purchased the Springburn Pottery, newly built by the bankrupt William McAdam and standing empty. At this works whiteware and stoneware were made under Currie with William D. Arnott as manager.

A fire damaged the old Works in Gallowgate in 1882 and it was closed down in 1885. The Springburn Works, however, functioned until 1899 when the Company went into voluntary liquidation. Its affairs were finally wound up in 1901.

No marked wares have ever been identified from any of the periods in the Gallowgate and of their nature it seems unlikely that any ever will be. From the whiteware period at Springburn many transfer-printed wares are known and some pieces of stoneware. The latter are well made and sometimes elaborate and salt-glazed. The Pottery made spongeware at this time but no marked specimens have been found.The transfer wares are not of the highest quality but are serviceable. Judging by modern distribution the pottery must have had quite a large trade with Ireland.

Pottery Description — printed: C.P.Co.Ltd.

Reading: Quail, G. "The Campbellfield Pottery" in *SPHR* 15 (1993): 27-42.

Pattern List:

Albany — a 'Japanese' pattern
Asiatic Pheasants — the usual
Broseley — the usual variant of Willow
Burns Centenary 1896
Cattle — cattle in a landscape
Chrysanthemum
Empress — same as the Verreville pattern
Imperial — a "Japanese" pattern with a large disc of black
Italia ?
Leopold
Mistletoe — birds perched on holly and mistletoe — a Christmas pattern
New Ivy
Panel Trefoil — on teaware
Ravenna — a lacustrine landscape
Rose

Scottish Lake
Seaside
Sport
Stag
Ta-Koo
Victoria
Waldeck
Willow — the usual
Youth

11.1. Two stoneware storage jars, approx. 8" ht. (£35/$60).

11.2. Pitcher: Rose, 7.25" ht. (£50/$85). Burns' Centenary 1896 bowl, 5.25" diam. (£40/$70). Bowl: Chrysanthemum, 4.5" ht. (£30/$50).

11.3. Plate: Willow, 8.5" (£20/$35). Platter: Asiatic Pheasant, 10" (£25/$40). Platter: Empress, 12" (£25/$40).

11.4. Pitcher: Leopold, 8" (£40/$70). Platter: Asiatic Pheasant, 16" lgth. (£60/$100).

12

Cleland Pottery, Cleland, Lanarkshire

Very little research has been carried out on the history of this Pottery. Even its opening and closing dates are not certain. The Pottery is shown on an Ordnance Survey map of 1896, so it must have been founded before this.

John Kennedy, younger son of Henry Kennedy of Barrowfield Pottery, left his partnership there and set up in the village of Cleland in Lanarkshire as a stoneware potter. The village lies in the heart of what was then a fruit-growing and jam-making area on the banks of the River Clyde and no doubt John hoped to capture the jam jar making trade of the area. This included both the one pound and two pound domestic jam jars and the more massive commercial variety.

He may well have succeeded for a time since, although the pottery was small the products are not scarce. They do not, however, stop at jam jars. The whole range of domestic and commercial wares is known, including ginger beer bottles and butter dishes. Some of the latter were made for the huge dairy empire of Lipton's. Mostly the pieces are of whitish body with an iron dip on the top part giving a two-tone effect. The pieces often bear the name of the customer for whom they were made and more lettering, printed in black. Limited use of rouletting was made, compared with other potteries. No elaborate wares have been reported from this Pottery.

The Works remained open at least until 1911 and cannot have remained open much beyond this since they are never mentioned in the papers of the Possil Pottery Board meetings, as all the functioning stoneware potteries are. But no firm closing date is known.

Cleland seems never to have made any but the most utilitarian of wares for commercial use.

Pottery Descriptions: Cleland Pottery Coy. Ld.

Reading: Askey, Derek *Stoneware Bottles* Brighton 1981: 196.

Cruickshank, Graeme "Cleland Pottery, Lanarkshire" in *SPHR* 5 (1980): 22-23.

12.1. Butter dish, 6.5" ht.(£45/$75) for Lipton's Dairies (These were made by several potteries). Ginger beer bottle, 7.5" ht.(£30/$50) and whisky flagon, 10" ht.(£35/$60).

12.2. Mark.

12.3. Butter dishes with retailers' names and addresses, approx. 6" ht.(£40-50/$70-85).

13

Clyde Pottery, Greenock

In the eighteenth century, the Clyde was too shallow for Glasgow to be a port for larger vessels. Glasgow's earliest solution to the problem was to build a port at the highest part of the Clyde navigable by sailing ships and to bring goods from the port to the town in flat boats called gabbarts. The port was known as Port Glasgow.

In the wake of this, the neighbouring landowner of Greenock estate quickly built his own port and, unrestricted in contrast with Port Glasgow with rules from the City, Greenock built itself into a prosperous town. It quickly captured the sugar refining industry from Glasgow but had shipbuilding and foreign trade on its own account also. Large fortunes were made in the town and the merchants were eventually faced with the same dilemma as Glasgow — a lack of manufactured goods to exchange for raw materials across the Atlantic.

In 1810 two merchants — James Muir and Alan Ker Jun. — joined with James Stevenson to form the Clyde Pottery on the south bank of the Clyde. Stevenson was a potter from Prestonpans in eastern Scotland. He had worked in Belfast in a creamware pottery and had had a china retail business in Greenock for some years in partnership with James Muir and his brother Andrew. He was appointed managing partner of the pottery, the other two supplied the capital. The Pottery had four kilns and housing for the workers and made creamware and pearlware. In 1823 the partners bought land high on the hill behind the town and built a flint mill on the banks of a stream.

Alan Ker's death in 1823 brought a crisis and the pottery was offered for sale but found no buyer. James Muir's death in 1834 brought an even greater crisis since he had willed that his businesses be sold off. His younger son Andrew and his brother, also Andrew, bought the pottery outright in 1836 and carried it on until 1841.

At this date the works was bought by an English potter, Thomas Shirley, and John Milligan, of whom little is known. Milligan disappeared from the scene very quickly and the firm was known as Thomas Shirley & Co., making white earthenware, mainly transfer printed.

Shirley died in 1850, leaving the pottery as a trust managed in effect by his son William. William was less than competent and ran the business at a loss until, after an unfortunate speculation with Larne Pottery in Northern Ireland, he became bankrupt in 1857. The Pottery was immediately taken over by a consortium of potters and businessmen who, with many changes of partnership, ran it successfully until 1904.

From the first period only one piece has been identified — a pearlware plaque with figures in Pratt colours, now in the Museum of Scotland in Edinburgh.

From the Andrew Muirs period we have only two transfer prints, both in blue: British Rivers and Caledonian. Both are conventional lacustrine landscapes. Caledonian is rather rare but has been found in the U.S.A. as well as in Scotland as dinner plates. British Rivers (13.1 & 13.2) was immensely popular and lasted certainly until the 1870s. It is a changing pattern and has been found on a great variety of dinner ware shapes. It is also known (13.1) with a centrepiece for a private commission.

From the Shirley period we have a much larger number of transfer patterns, all of them conventional lacustrine landscapes. British Rivers continued and a new pattern — Gondola — proved popular enough to last well into the next period, on mugs, pitchers and punch bowls (13.3). Whereas the Muir period is known only from dinner wares, the range of shapes from the Shirley period is somewhat greater, including mugs, pitchers and teaware. The Shirley mark (13.4 & 5) often includes a beehive, a motif which was carried on for a short time into the next period.

The Clyde Pottery Company took very little time to get into its stride, producing a vast variety of wares in a large number of very varied transfer prints as well as some moulded, some painted and some spongeware. British Rivers survived and was produced in huge amounts well into the life of the Company (13.6). One or two other patterns survived less successfully (13.7) bearing the beehive mark with C.P.Co. substituted for T.S. & Co. (13.8). Sometimes the changing of the mark was not so well accomplished, as in Oriental Scene(ry) where T.S. & Co. has been imperfectly obliterated and C.P.Co.

engraved on top, giving the impression of a pottery called T.C.P. & Co.(13.43, 44). One jug in a new shape (13.7) with a painted blue tree was copied from English originals. This is known variously as 'the Glasgow jug' and 'the Fife jug' but there is no convincing evidence for manufacture in either of these centres and it seems likely that Clyde was the only Scottish maker.

Moulded wares include openwork baskets (13.9) and various pitchers (13.10). One of these is a very accurate copy of a Bells' parian pitcher; another shows an overall hunting scene.

Dinner wares include Willow and a pattern called Washington, presumably meant for export (13.11). Other pitcher shapes were made (13.12), including one (13.13-19) which proved very popular indeed. Punch bowls were made, often in patterns which occur also on pitchers.

The patterns in the first part of this period show an enormous increase in range and very quickly the lacustrine landscape becomes a thing of the past. The wedding of the Prince of Wales to Princess Alexandra of Denmark in June 1863 was commemorated on a pitcher, a punch bowl and a tobacco jar, all in the same pattern but called Royal Jug, Royal Bowl or nothing respectively (13.15). Valentine shows a Cupid delivering a letter to a young girl and is obviously meant as a gift for a sweetheart (13.16). King William III was produced for members of the Orange Order (13.18). Prince Charlie was simply a piece of patriotism (13.15) and My Pet was for the sentimentally inclined (13.17).

Around 1875 the output of the pottery changed completely. Old shapes and patterns were scrapped and new ones introduced. Pitchers were once again the dominant product with small bowls a poor second. A donation made to the local Museum on its inception in 1877 shows some very untypical pieces, some in mazarin blue and some showing elaborate goldwork, probably from the showroom. Teacups, feature some moulds and cut sponges for sponge-printing. One not very successful pitcher shape is known (13.19) in just two patterns. Rose is the first in a long series named for and showing young girls. Spunky shows dogs teaching a puppy to kill rats!

Another pitcher shape, featured in the donation to the McLean Museum (13.20 — 24), was more successful. Patterns known include one (13.24) for a well-known sporting personality, or perhaps a horse. It is in this shape that a long series of painted jugs is first found. The painting featured is robust but was very popular and is often to be found after 1880 combined with a pink or a pale blue stripe (13.31, 34). The usual subject is flowers (13.31, 35) but more patriotic themes sometimes appear (13.27) and occasionally religious motifs. The enamelling was done above the glaze and has often worn from use. One unique transfer print celebrated a birthday (13.24).

The series of young girls continues with Gerty, Florence, Mae, Ada, Sylph and Mary (13.25, 26, 30, 33). Christmas pitchers were produced in great numbers. Sometimes they were simply the usual patterns with an added inscription or a band of holly but from time to time they were specially for the season (13.26, 30). A commemorative pattern was made for the Glasgow International Exhibition of 1888 and used on pitchers, punch bowls and cheese dishes (13.2). Especially popular patterns include Cottage, Tam O'Shanter, and The Lily of the Valley. The last is found on dinner ware, pitchers, porringers, chamber pots and punch bowls in black, pink or blue/green, plain or clobbered (13.37).

Towards the end of the pottery's life a number of pieces are found decorated with a hand-painted pink rose, known locally as the Murray Rose since tradition has it that it was painted by a Mr. Murray who lived in the pottery. It has been assumed that all pieces with the Murray Rose, though unmarked, were made at Clyde Pottery. This is questionable for a number of reasons. Murray worked independently of the pottery and continued until the 1930s. His wife was head painter at the pottery and conceivably could have executed the wares in her spare time (13.36).

Dinner wares were not totally ignored. Grecian (13.38) was produced in both lilac and grey; Chariot was probably bought when Annfield Pottery closed in the 1880s and printed thereafter in black (13.39). Various others were made in black or light blue (13.40). One — Contest — seems to have been popular since it appears, not just on dinner wares but on punch bowls and porringers (13.41). Cottage was revived in a slightly different form with rustic frames towards the end of the pottery's life when standards were slipping slightly (13.42).

Throughout this period spongeware was made but has largely been unattributed through a total lack of marked pieces. One fairly common set of patterns is known from sherds found during an excavation on the site. This shows butterflies in brown or black and sometimes a fleur de lis. It is clobbered in red and green and sometimes also in yellow and blue. One pitcher shape presents a slight problem. Dating from the 1860s and early 1870s, it is undoubtedly a Clyde Pottery mould since it exists in large numbers and with a large number of Clyde patterns—usually marked; however, specimens are known with patterns which belong to the Links Pottery in Kirkcaldy and which even bear its mark. Links patterns include Roman (13.41) and Butterfly (25.5). Other patterns, e.g. Pepu, are known with no pottery description at all. One possibility is that Links ordered Clyde blanks under pressure of orders and decorated them themselves. This is made more likely in that Butterfly is known on definite Links shapes. Again, the matter remains open.

Clyde Pottery began as did so many Scottish potteries by aiming quite high in the market and exporting creamware widely; but, over the years its market became more and more humble and it ended as a provider of pitchers for ordinary housewives. This points up a problem for all Scottish potteries. The home market for quality wares was so small that the only alternatives were success in the export market, such as was obtained by Bells', Britannia, Methven's and Fife or a descent into supplying their local market as happened to Clyde and Victoria.

Pottery Descriptions: Greenock Pottery — incised
A.M. — transfer
T.S. & Co. or Coy. — transfer
C.P.Co. or Coy. — transfer
Clyde P. Co. — transfer
Clyde Pottery — transfer

Reading: Boa, et al. *The Clyde Pottery* — Greenock (1987) [caution: this work contains serious inaccuracies].

Denholm, P. "Pottery Excavations: their problems and products" in *Scottish Archaeological Forum* 8 (1976): 37-51.

Kelly, H.E. "The Beginning of the pottery Industry in Greenock" in *Scottish Industrial History* 17 (1994): 57-75.

— "The Wares of the Clyde Pottery Co." in *SPHR* 13 (1988/9): 39-73.

— "The Jugs of the Clyde Pottery Co." in *SPHR* 10 (1985/6): 25-30 [these last two are now slightly out of date].

Pattern List:

The patterns have been grouped by period, ignoring differences in pottery descriptions which do not seem to have any significance for dating. Where there is no description, the pattern is illustrated.

Muir period:
British Rivers
Caledonian — lacustrine landscape with horse rider in foreground.

Shirley period:
Aleppo
Athenian Sketches
Broseley
Continental Cathedrals
Foughabellagh — known only from sherd found in dig.
Gondola
Mansion — lacustrine landscape
Oriental Scenes or Scenery
Rio
Saxon
Le Tombeau de Paul et Virginia
Venetian Sketches — lacustrine landscape

Clyde Pottery Company:
Ada
Aquatic — lake with fish and castle on island
Birds — two birds on nest
Bouquet — flowers hanging from a ribbon — never marked
British Rivers
Cable — a cable
Cabul
Canton — illustrated here but never marked
Chariot
Claremont — fruit and flowers
Clyde — floral
Contest — never marked but illustrated here
Cottage
Delhi
Floral — floral
Florence
French
Gem
Gerty
Glasgow Exhibition 1888

13.1. British Rivers - A.M. - a changing pattern with one specimen of a private commission. Commissioned plate, 10.25" diam. (£80/$135). Platters, 15.50", 13" (£150, 100/$170, 250). Other plates, 10.50" diam. (£60/$100).

Gondola
Gothic
Grapes — a bunch of grapes, later made by Possil Pottery
Grecian
Hawthorn Blosssom
Heather — heather sprig
Heather Bell
Indian Tree
Iona
Ivy
Japanese
Joy — children and flowers
Jubilee
Lahore
The Lily of the Valley
Louise — known from just one sherd.
Mae
Mario
Mary
May Flower
Melrose — floral
Moresque — abstract
My Pet
Oriental
Oriental Scenes or Scenery
Passion Flower — a passion flower
Peace
Pekin
Prince Charlie
Procession — a line of figures round a bowl
Rose
Rosebery
Royal Bowl
Royal Jug
Royal Stag — seems to be identical to Stag
Shield
Stag — see Royal Stag
Sydney — plant abstract
Sylph
Tam O' Shanter
Valentine
Vase — a vase
Washington
Willow
Windsor — floral
York — floral
Zephyr

13.2. British Rivers - A.M. - (r.) 13.50" diam. (£60/$100) and Le Tombeau de Paul et Virginia (T.S. & Co.) (l.) 10.50" diam. (£60/$100).

13.4 - 13.5. T.S. & Co. beehive marks.

13.3. Plates: Continental Cathedrals (l.) and Rio (r.) 10.75" diam. (£40/$70 each). Pitchers: Aleppo (l.) 8" ht. and Saxon (r.) 6.50" ht. (£70/$120 each). Mugs: Gondola, approx. 5" ht.(£55/$90 each). Cup & saucer: Broseley, 4.75" cup diam. (£35/$60). All T.S. & Co.

13.6. British Rivers in various forms - c. P.Co. Platter, 13.75" lgth. (£60/$100). Tureen, 13.50" diam. (£40/$70). Plates, 10.75" & 9.75" diam. (£25/$40 each).

13.7. Bowls: the Chinese porringer is unmarked while the other bears the mark shown in photo 13.8. Pitchers: plain white, sheet pattern, French, Glasgow jug, French with clobbering. Bowls, 7" diam. (£35/$60 each). Pitchers, 9" ht. (£40-60/$70-100).

13.8. Possible P.Co. beehive mark.

13.9. Basket with moulded gondola, c. P.Co impressed ship mark, 12.75" lgth. (£120/$200).

13.10. Moulded pitchers: two with overall hunting scene, 7" ht. and one blue, 8.75" copied from Bells' original — all with c. P.Co ship mark (£100/$170).

13.11. Plates: Willow, Washington. Pitchers: Oriental and Gondola — all c. P.Co. Plates, 10.75" diam. (£25/$40). Pitchers, approx. 7.50" ht. (£35-60/$60-100).

13.12. Plates: Gothic and Ivy in mulberry with c. P.Co. ship marks. Pitchers: Spring, one with inscription for 1860 — c. P.Co. Plates, 10.75" diam. (£35/$60). Pitchers, 8.50" ht. (£50/$85).

13.13. Plates: Lahore with c. P.Co. ship mark. Pitcher: Indian Tree. Punch bowl: Spring - both c. P.Co. Plates, 7.25" & 6.50" diam. (£20/$35). Pitcher, 8.50" ht. (£50/$85). Punch bowl, 10" diam. (£90/$150).

13.14. Spring mark.

13.15. Pitcher: Prince Charlie, the rest for the Royal wedding of 1863 — c. P.Co. Pitchers, 8.50" ht. (£65, 140/$110, 235). Punch bowl, 9.75" diam. (£160/$270). Tobacco jar (£60/$100).

13.16. Pitcher: Valentine — c. P.Co., 8.50" ht. (£80/ $135).

13.17. Pitchers: Peace (2), French and My Pet — all c. P.Co., 8.50" ht. (£35/$60 each).

13.18. Pitcher: Canton — unmarked, 8.50" ht. (£40/$70). Cup & saucer: King William III - unmarked (£65/$110). Ewer: Heather Bell — c. P.Co., 12.50" ht. (£50/ $85).

13.19. Pitchers: Spunky, Rose, 7.50" ht. (£50-80/$85-135). Porringer: Gem, 5.50" diam. (£25/$40) — all c. P.Co.

13.20. Impressed ship mark in use from 1857 - c. 1870.

13.21. Pitchers: Stag, 8.50" ht. (£50/$85 each). Punchbowl: Cabul, 9.75" diam. (£120/$200) — all c. P.Co.

13.22. Pitchers: Japanese, 8.50" ht. (£45/$75). Porringer: Pekin, 6.25" diam. (£30/$50) — both c. P.Co.

13.23. Pitchers: Cherry Ripe, Zephyr, 8.50" ht. (£50/$85 each) — both c. P.Co. Porringer, 6" diam. unmarked (£30/$50).

13.24. Pitchers: painted, moulded, birthday, Rosebery, Mario — 8.50" ht., the last two c. P.Co. (£35-100/ $60-170).

13.25. Gerty, Florence (side 1), Mae — c. P.Co. or Clyde P.Co., 7.50" & 8" ht. (£50-90/$85-150).

13.26. Pitchers with Christmas patterns: boys throwing snowballs (which are added pellets of clay) [unmarked], Florence (side 2), Ada, fashion jug [both sides, one with holly, one with blue stripe.]. Mostly c. P.Co., 8" & 8.25" ht. (£60-100/$100-170).

13.27. Pitcher: painted, 8" ht. (£30/$50). Cheese dish and pitcher for Glasgow International Exhibition of 1888 — no marks, 10.50" & 8" ht. (£120, 150/$200, 250).

13.28. Cottage - Clyde Pottery. Pitchers, 8" ht. (£40-55/$70-90). Bowl, 6.25" diam. (£30/$50).

13.29. Mark for Cottage.

13.30. Sylph, plain and clobbered as Christmas jug — c. P.Co. Pitchers, 8" ht. (£35-60/$60-100). Plate, 10.50" diam. (£50/$85).

13.31. Painted pitchers — unmarked, 8.25" ht. (£20-30/$30-50).

13.32. Tam O'Shanter — Clyde Pottery. Pitchers, 8.25" ht. (£35/$60 each). Bowl, 6" diam. (£35/$60). Plaque, 9" diam. (£80/135).

13.33. Pitchers: Ada and two forms of Mary, 8.25" ht. (£35-70/$60-120).

13.34. Painted pitchers — unmarked, 8.25" ht. (£30-35/$50-60).

13.35. Painted pitchers — unmarked, 8.25" ht.(£20-35/$35-60).

13.36. The Murray Rose on a plate and two pitchers, one certainly made at Clyde Pottery. Pitchers, 7.50", 8.25" ht. (£50/$85). Plate, 9" diam. (£30/$50).

13.37. The Lily of the Valley — c. P.Co. Pitcher, 8.25" ht. (£35/$60). Plate (£20/$35). Bowl, 6.50" diam. (£20/$35).

13.38. Plate and platter: 10" & 11" diam. Grecian (£25, 30/$40, 50). Teaplate: Delhi — all c. P.Co., 8.25" diam. (£20-30/$35-50).

13.39. Plate and platter: Chariot — J.T. and c. P.Co.,10.50" & 11" (£25, 30-$40, 50). Bowls: Hawthorn Blossom — c. P.Co., 5.25" diam. (£30/$50).

Opposite page:
Top: 13.40. Teaplate and saucer: Shield — Clyde Pottery, 7.50" & 5.75" diam. (£20, 10/$35, 17). Back row centre: the plate is Empress from Campbellfield Pottery — c. P.Co. Ltd. Front two plates: May Flower and Iona — c. P.Coy., both 9.50" diam. (£20/$35).

Bottom: 13.41. Contest as platter, punch bowl and porringer. Pitcher: Roman — D.M. & SS, i.e. Links Pottery, Kirkcaldy. Platter, 14" lgth. (£35, 60). Punch bowl, 10" diam. (£80/$135). Pitcher, 8" ht. (£80/$135). Bowl, 6.25" diam. (£30/$50).

13.42. Chamber pots: The Lily of the Valley and Cottage in ts revised form. 9.25" diam. (£50/$90).

13.43. Plate: Oriental Scenery. c. 1857, 10.50" diam. (£30/$50).

13.43a. Mark.

13.44. Two punch bowls. Left: probably Clyde — right: Clyde — both 10.25" diam. (£80/$135).

14

Cumnock Pottery, Cumnock, Ayrshire

The moving spirits in the foundation of this redware Pottery were the Countess of Dumfries and her agent James Taylor, who before this had been involved in early experiments with the adaptation of James Watt's engine to steamships and with prospecting for and mining metals. In 1794 Lady Dumfries engaged two potters from Glasgow to set up a Pottery on the estate to work clay which had been found there. Taylor was to have a half share in this business, partly on his own account and partly for the Earl of Dumfries. The Glasgow potters proved useless and the pottery was closed for two years.

Taylor then re-opened the Works solely as a country redware pottery making the usual range of wares for that period. It is unlikely that Taylor ever made a profit from the pottery and, having struggled for years against mounting debts, he died on 18 September 1825, aged 67.

His son Robert took over the running of the Works in 1826 but withdrew in 1837. In 1838 a lease was taken by a lawyer called Alexander Hamilton as Cumnock Pottery & Tile Co., but only until 1839. He modernised the Works and expanded the manufacture of ornamental ware started by Robert Taylor, but died very suddenly in 1839. For a period the pottery was run by his widow and trustees.

In 1852, J.M. Nicol became manager, proprietor in 1856 and after his death in 1885 the pottery was run by members of his family until 1906 when it finally closed down.

Cumnock's wares look more monotonous than they should since only motto wares can be attributed with any certainty. The difficulty arises, as it does with most country potteries, because the everyday wares were never marked, being destined for no greater a fate than to be used until they broke and then to be thrown away. Any survivals have long ago been bought by dealers and sold off as coming from more fashionable country potteries and we are left with motto wares. The only clue to anything else is that the body of Cumnock's wares is mottled which seems to be characteristic. The most ambitious pieces ever made were salt buckets with a nesting bird on top, the nest being made from clay "worms". These are rare and extremely sought after by collectors.

The earliest piece known is in the Baird Institute in Cumnock. It is a flagon with a patch of white slip and a sgrafitto dedication including the date 1801. At a later date, probably under the Nicols, a decorative ware known as Scotch Motto Ware was made. For this, part of the piece was covered with white slip and a couthy motto in broad Scots was scratched through this in sgraffito. This was extremely popular and was widely imitated by Alloa Pottery, by Dunmore and by the Torquay potteries of South Devon. Many shapes were made including frog mugs and more useful models. As well as this, salt buckets were made with tulips slip-trailed on them or with other patterns. A few pieces are known with yellow slip all over. Late in the life of the Pottery some experimental pieces were made but they were not successful.

Pottery Descriptions: Cumnock Pottery — incised and rare.

Reading: Quail, G. "The Cumnock Pottery — Ayrshire." *A & NHSoc* 1993

______. "The Foundation of the Cumnock Pottery." in *SPHR* 17 (1995): 27-29.

14.1. Salt bucket with typical Cumnock tulips, 10.25" ht. (£100/$170); tumbler, 2.75" ht. (£30/50), pitcher, 6.50" ht. (£60/$100) and bowl, 6.75" diam. (£20/$35), all with mottoes.

14.2. Salt bucket of heavier make and different design, 12" ht. (£60/$100), tobacco jars, 4.50" ht. (£50/$85) and sugar basins, 2.50" ht. (£15/$25) with mottoes.

14.3. Bowls with rustic handles, 8" diam. (£70/$120), frog mug, 4" ht. (£60/$100) and smaller pieces, 2' - 4.25" (£10-15/$17-25), all with mottoes. The bowl with green slip (4.25" diam.) has the well-known Selkirk Grace:
SOME HAE MEAT THAT CANNA EAT
AN' SOME WAD EAT THAT WANT IT
BUT WE HAE MEAT AN' WE CAN EAT
AN' SAE THE LORD BE THANKIT.

15

Delftfield Pottery, Glasgow

By the middle of the eighteenth century, Glasgow merchants felt the need to provide manufactured goods for the American market to form part of the cycle of trade which they had set up around the Atlantic. Tobacco (and later cotton) from Virginia, rum and sugar from the Caribbean, and slaves from West Africa were other major factors in the cycle.

In 1748 four Glasgow merchants formed the Glasgow Delft Company to manufacture delftware and bought a site just to the west of Glasgow. The four were Lawrence and Robert Dinwiddie, Robert Finlay and Patrick Nisbet. The Dinwiddies were brothers: Lawrence—an ex-Lord Provost of the city, Robert—a prosperous merchant in London who was shortly thereafter to be made Lieutenant-Governor of Virginia. He it was who sent a defence of the British possession of Ohio to General Saint Pierre in the hands of Major George Washington, whose first important commission this was.

The founding of the Delftfield Pottery was the initiation of the Scottish commercial pottery industry. Robert recruited London potters who were contracted to train Scots in the business. After some initial difficulties, both technical and legal, the Delftfield Pottery began to produce large quantities of ware, most of which was exported to areas across the Atlantic Ocean.

The choice of delft as their ware's body was odd, since delft was already giving way to white salt-glazed stoneware and creamware in the English potteries north of Bristol and London. The advent of the celebrated James Watt as a partner resulted in the Company manufacturing white stoneware, creamware, pearlware, coloured wares and china. The creamware was to a formula invented by James Watt himself.

There were many changes of partner over the years until, in 1823, the Pottery bought and merged with the Caledonian Pottery in north Glasgow, moving to their premises and from then on its history is that of the Caledonian.

Only one marked piece from the Delftfield Pottery has ever been found. This is a pearlware model of a church, now in Glasgow Museums' collection. All other pieces can be attributed only on stylistic or provenencal grounds. There have been several excavations on or near the site of this Pottery as well as the recovery of sherds from trenches dug nearby when utility companies carried out repairs and a large selection of sherds is known in several bodies. Some of these have been published by the Scottish Pottery Society in their Review. The delft wares are now represented in museums all over Europe and North America since delft is so greatly prized by collectors. Only one or two pieces of creamware have probable attributions to the pottery (15.1). The Glasgow Art Galleries and Museums collection includes some pieces of porcelain and black basalte which may well have been made by Delftfield.

Pottery Descriptions: only one is known — it is an incised Delftfield with a date in 1786.

Reading: Denholm, P. "Mid eighteenth century tin-glazed earthenware from the Defltfield Pottery Glasgow" in *Post-Mediaeval Archaeology* 16 (1982)

Kelly, H.E. "Documents relating to Delftfield" in *SPHR* 15 (1993): 43-50.

King horn, J. & Quail, G. *Delftfield* — Glasgow 1986 — Glasgow Museums.

Quail, G. "James Watt of Delftfield" and "More Pieces of Glasgow Delftware" — both in *SPHR6* (1981): 44-54 & 64-66.

______. "More Delftfield sherds" in *SPHR* 7 (1982): 58-65.

15.1. Creamware punch bowl with Scottish Masonic Arms and remains of painted swags of flowers. Probably Delftfield, 11.50" diam. (£1500/$2500).

16

Drongan Pottery, Drongan, Ayrshire

With the growth of mining in the Ayrshire coalfields in the early 19th century came the discovery of associated pockets of high quality red clay suitable for making earthenware ground-drainage tiles and other forms of redware. Since Ayrshire farmers and landowners were intent at this time on draining the land as an essential part of their agricultural improvements, this discovery was very timely. However, even the enormous output of some of the tile works founded at this time could not keep up with the demand. In spite of this, a few of these works developed into full-blown potteries and specialised in making dairy wares and a number of other types for general use. The best known of these are Cumnock and Drongan, which lay within a few miles of each other and close to the county town and port of Ayr.

There may have been a pottery on the site of the Drongan Works in the 18th century but the redware Pottery we know was founded in 1832 by Robert Boyle, who was born nearby in 1803 to a potter father. Drongan was perhaps not Robert's first pottery and was certainly not his only business. His headquarters were in Ayr where he lived and from his office there he ran a brickworks also. The Bank tilework was opened in 1837 and was sold in 1846 to Archibald Hamilton, owner of the Rozelle Estate. For him, Boyle took down the tile work and transported it to nearby Carncluie, where it was rebuilt to make tiles for Archibald Hamilton.

Boyle was a thorough entrepreneur and by 1845 was advertising an invention of his own in combination with John Young, an engineer of Ayr. This was a machine for turning out up to 20, 000 tiles per day with the help of 2 men and 5 boys. By this time Boyle had a widespread trade going all over south-west Scotland but also to Wales and Ireland and, according to him, to the U.S.A. For the last there is no evidence except his own statement but the Irish and Welsh connections are certain and he is known to have imported Welsh slate for roofing.

However, by 1851 Boyle and his family were living at the Drongan Pottery site and by 1861 he was in deep financial trouble. His tile machine had lost money and he had engaged in speculative building on the outskirts of Ayr, using borrowed capital. He had lost at least one cargo by the disappearance of the ship carrying it. By November 1863 he was declared bankrupt and by April 1865 the pottery was closed and the stock and machinery sold off. Nothing more is known of Boyle.

No marked pieces of Drongan's wares have ever been found, though there is a rumour of one piece in a museum in New Zealand. But many sherds have been rescued from building trenches on the site and there has been a small dig there which also found sherds and uncovered part of a kiln.

The quality of the body is very high, so the clay obtained from behind the pottery site must also have been of high quality. Drainpipes of the tubular kind and of the two-piece kind must always have been the principal source of income, but all kinds of dairy ware and the usual redwares were made such as jelly cans, porringers, wash pans, pickle dishes, honey pots, crocks, etc.

Pieces were decorated occasionally with rouletting but the favoured form of decoration used slip. White slip was trailed over brown or brown over white, white slip was sometimes trailed over the biscuit pot or a mixture of slips was marbled on the surface. Black-glazed wares were also made in abundance. Most of the categories described would never have been marked by a country pottery anywhere in Europe or North America, which makes identifying their source next to impossible.

Reading: Kelly, H.E. "Drongan Pottery" in *SPHR* 16 (1994): 11-22.
______. "The Broomberrry Tileworks and Robert Boyle" in *SPHR* 19(1998): 11-14.
Retter, Janet. *Drongan, the story of a Mining Village* - The Baird Institute, Cumnock (1978).

16.1. Sherds found on the site of the Pottery during building work.

17

Dunmore Pottery, Dunmore, Stirlingshire

Dunmore Pottery was situated south of the town of Alloa on the estate of the Earl of Dunmore. The date of its origin in uncertain since it was for its first period simply a country pottery using local clays to form the usual utilitarian items of crockery for domestic and dairy use.

In 1866, however, Peter Gardner took over the pottery on the death of his father, John. Where Peter Gardner trained as a potter is still a mystery. It must have been somewhere where majolica was made since this is the type of ware he chose to make from then on. At first he used local clay, which was of a high quality, but later he imported clays from Devon and Cornwall in England.

The Countess of Dunmore is said to have taken a great interest in the pottery, bringing the Prince of Wales on a visit in 1871 and even designing shapes for some of the pots. Queen Victoria is said to have bought a large number of pieces at the Edinburgh Exhibition of 1886 and there was a particularly grand exhibit at the 1888 International Exhibition in Glasgow.

A local newspaper published a detailed description of a visit to the pottery around 1885, picturing the making of a teapot from beginning to end.

When Peter Gardner retired, the business was bought by a Robert Henderson, who shortly thereafter sold to Thomas Harrison, who was a potter from a potting family with wide connections in England. He died in 1912 but his widow carried on until c.1917 when the pottery was closed.

Dunmore is celebrated and widely collected for its ornamental wares. Teapots, vases and pitchers are found in great numbers but along with them are rustic and grotesque pieces (17.5, 6). Cauldrons, woven baskets, shoes, fruit and animals are found, toads being a particular favourite amongst the last. These are sometimes of a fairly large size and remind one somewhat of the Martin Brothers grotesque birds.

But it is the glazes which make Dunmore Pottery. Gardner was perpetually experimenting. A bluish green was a favourite but browns, reds, blues, greens, yellows, and turquoises are also found, as well as other colours. Glazes are mottled, mixed, crackled and splashed with great assurance.

Unfortunately no work has yet been done on a chronology of shapes or of glazes, so the pieces exist in a chronological void.

Pottery Descriptions: impressed

Dunmore
Dunmore Pottery
Peter Gardner Dunmore Pottery

Reading: "Dunmore Pottery" — Anon. A reprint of a newspaper article by the Central Branch of the Scottish Pottery Society.

Dickson, Kay. "Dunmore" — paper read to Scottish Pottery Society Glasgow Branch March 1985 — Summarised in Newsletter.

17.1. Large pot, 7.50" ht., vase, 6" ht. and ink well, 7" diam. disguised as a pear on a plate (£80, 40, 100/$135, 70, 170).

17.2. Mark on ink well.

17.3. Wall plaque, 11.75" diam. (£500/$835).

17.4. Large moulded jar, 9.50" ht. (£500/$835)

17.5. Grotesques, 3"-5.75" ht. (£250/$420 each).

17.7. Animals, 2.75" - 6" ht. (£60-100/ $100-170 each).

17.6. Mythical beasts, including a very rare bird, 5" - 7" ht. (£80-400/ $135-670).

17.8. Multiple vases, 7.25" - 13.75" ht. (£200/$340 each).

17.9. Large ornamental pitcher, 17" ht. (£400/ $670).

17.10. Fruit and bonbon dishes, 8" - 8.50" diam. (£50/$85 each).

17.11. Handled vases, 5.75" - 7" ht. (£80-200/ $135-340 each).

17.12. Copies of Cumnock motto ware: left-hand piece, 4.25" ht. (£100-140/$170-235 each).

17.13. Large classical urn, 26" ht. (£3500/$590).

17.14. Impressed mark.

17.15. Moulded game dish, 11.75" lgth. (£550/$920).

17.16. Ornamental ware, 7.75" - 12.50" ht. (£60, 100/$100, 170).

17.17. Lady Dunmore vase, 12" lgth. (£100/$170).

17.18. Rare looking glass, 16" diam (£600/$1020)

17.20. Ornamental ware, 9" ht. (£100/$170).

17.19. Classical vases, 12.50" - 13.25" ht. (£100/$170).

17.21. Mug, tea kettle and ornamental dish: tea kettle, 7.50" ht. (£100-200/$170-340).

17.22. Baskets and bottle: baskets, 6" ht. (£200/$340).

17.23. Mottled glazes: centre top, 7" ht.; leaf, 10.25" diam. (£80-100/$135-170).

17.24. Ornamental wares, 5.25" - 11.50" ht. (£90-120/$150-200).

17.25. Vases, 11" - 13" ht. (£100/$170).

18

Eagle Pottery, Glasgow

Frederick Grosvenor, who founded this Pottery, was born in Hanley in Staffordshire in 1833. From 1833 until 1860, his life is a blank but in the latter year he married the daughter of an Edinburgh businessman, so was probably already in Scotland. His next appearances are in 1864 as leaving the Glasgow Glass Bottle Co. and as a partner in the Caledonian Pottery as Murrays & Grosvenor. It is not known why he came to Glasgow, how he obtained his capital, nor how he trained in the pottery business unless the last was the reason for his joining the partnership.

In 1868 the partnership was dissolved and Frederick, having looked at land in Grangemouth and at the Clyde Pottery, bought land in the east end of Glasgow in the district of Bridgeton and founded the Bridgeton Pottery in 1869. By 1870 he was affluent enough to buy a large terraced house near the pottery to house his growing family.

He had an extremely clear and active brain and various improvements in the making of stoneware were patented by him in 1870, 1881, 1884, 1888 and 1911. The Pottery grew and eventually had 12 kilns. In 1882 its name was changed to the Eagle Pottery and a stylised eagle was sometimes used as a trade mark, often moulded or impressed on the base.

Frederick's son Donald became a partner in 1889 and the firm became Grosvenor & Son. In 1892 Frederick was the director of the Potters' Federation Ltd. — Donald had his turn as chairman in 1900. Frederick was chairman in 1904 at a retirement party for A.W. Buchan and A. Gray of Portobello. In 1905 the pottery had a fire in the jolley and throwing shops but was quickly rebuilt in an art nouveau style.

After Frederick's death in 1915, Donald ran the pottery. He has been credited with allowing the pottery to go to seed but the decades from 1910 to the 1930s were a period of decline for all stoneware potteries since glass or rubber were replacing stoneware in many of its functions. The Pottery closed in 1923 but the buildings stood until 1994 when they were finally demolished. Donald lived on till 1945.

Eagle's wares were the usual domestic and commercial stonewares: whisky flagons (18.3, 5), beer bottles, acid jars and butter pots (18.4, 5) as well as bird waterers (18.5), baskets and water filters. They also made earthenware teapots and jugs (18.10). The stoneware had a borax glaze; the teapots, a brown Rockingham glaze. All the wares were of good quality and well designed. At least one piece of terra cotta is known to have been made. It is a very lifelike, but less than life size, male head with a ventilating hole in the top and another in the corner of the mouth, presumably for the insertion of a 'cutty' or claypipe (18.10). Latterly, under Donald Grosvenor, the firm made electrical insulators.

Pottery Descriptions: Grosvenor

Grosvenor & Son

Reading: Quail G. "The Bridgeton or Eagle Pottery." in *SPHR* 10 (1986): 22-24.

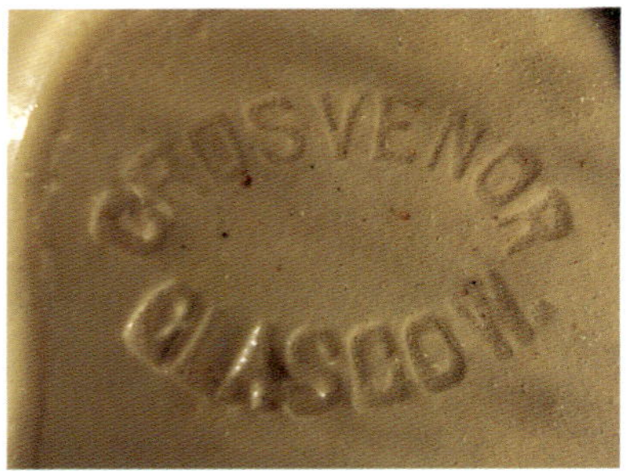

18.2. Mark.

18.1. Storage jars, 5.25" and 8.25" ht. (£35-40/$60-70 each).

18.3. Stoneware pitcher (£45/$75), bottle, 5" ht. (£15/$25) and whisky flagon, 5.50" ht. (£60/$100).

18.4. Butter dishes (£40-50/$70-85) and flour bin in stoneware (£60/$100).

18.5. Butter dish, 5.25" ht.(£40/$70), small flagon, 4" ht.(£30/$50) and bird waterer, 12.50" ht.(£90/$150).

18.6. Two tobacco jars, 11" ht. (£150/$250 the pair).

18.7. Two whisky barrels, 12.75" and 16.50" ht. (£80-90/$135-150).

18.8. Casserole, 13.50" lgth. (£90/$150).

18.9. Casserole, 15" lgth. and two storage jars, 10.50" ht. A set made specially as a wedding present. They are unmarked but attributed to Eagle due to the casserole's similarity to the one shown in 18.8 (£180/$300). A special mould had to be made for the inscription so the present was regal.

18.10. Rockingham glazed teapot, 7.50" ht.(£50/$85) and pitcher (£60/$100) with terra cotta head, 6.50" ht. (£50/$85).

19

Elgin and Mile-End Potteries, Glasgow

The founder of the Elgin Pottery was James Johnston, a grocer in the Calton district of Glasgow's east end. In 1855 he formed a partnership with William Reid, a potter from nearby Annfield Pottery, Joseph Vaughan, also a potter, and James Sellar, a smith. The Pottery was in the same area of the Calton and must have been successful in the manufacture of Bristol and saltglaze stoneware since in 1857 they expanded. But the partners had overstretched their finances and were declared bankrupt in October 1860. John Hurll, a fire clay manufacturer, and John Lyon of the Mountainblue Pottery were creditors at this time.

The works were put up for sale and bought by Charles Purvis or Purves, a potter, for £370. The Purvises were a family of potters who had a strong connection with the Verreville Pottery the Cochran family who owned it and the Britannia Pottery. William Reid, from the old partnership, joined Charles Purvis briefly but left in 1861 and Purvis carried on alone. The Works switched over to making white earthenware with transfer-printed decoration and was successful enough for Charles to sell the pottery in 1867 to his brother Thomas for £2000. Charles went further east to a bigger works.

Thomas had put a strain on his finances from the first. He converted to making Firestone teapots with a Rockingham glaze. These had a fireclay grog and could be heated to quite a high temperature without breaking, so they were quite successful. But Thomas had to borrow money to continue and in May 1875 was declared bankrupt. The Pottery was sold to be the stable for a tramway company.

Meanwhile in 1867, on his move to the east, Charles Purvis had built the Mile-End Pottery in partnership with John Denny. Denny was a member of a well-known family of shipbuilders from Dumbarton. From whatever motives Denny had joined the partnership, he left the following year. This, and the fact that Charles Purvis had borrowed £700 from Robert Cochran of Verreville and Britannia Potteries, must have put a strain on the financial situation. Operations seem to have stopped in 1877 but at this time Alexander Cochran, son of Robert and now owner of Britannia, took a ten year lease on the Works. Whether the pottery produced anything at that time is not known, nor is the final date of closure.

The reason for writing of these two potteries together is that their outputs were small and are not always distinguishable since a common mark 'C.P.' was used.

No marked wares have been found from the Johnstone period and only a teapot sherd from the Thomas Purvis period. Plates and lidded vegetable dishes in a blue and white pattern called 'Windsor' are quite commonly found (19.1). Some are marked C.P. Elgin Pottery and some are marked P.D. & Co. for Purvis, Denny & Co.; however, some are marked N.B. Pottery for the North British Pottery, who probably bought the copper plates for the transfer when Mile-End closed. A number of pitchers are known, marked simply 'C.P.' It is not known whether these came from Elgin or Mile-End. Much of the information in this chapter comes from a privately printed article on Elgin Pottery by G. Quail.

Pottery Descriptions: C.P. Elgin Pottery — printed
P.D. & Co. — printed
C.P. — printed
Thomas Purves firestone Elgin Pottery — impressed

Reading: Kelly, H.E. "The Life of Robert Cochran of Britannia and Verreville Potteries" in *Scottish Industrial History* 18 (1996): 8-20. This is not particularly relevant but has information on the connection of the Purvis and Cochran families.

Pattern List:
Iris — flowers.
The Shepherd Boy — boy with sheep in landscape.
Windsor — a lacustrine landscape with an avenue of gigantic statues.

19.1. Serving dish with lid, printed with Windsor, 11" diam. (£35/$60).

20

Fife or Gallatoun Pottery

The Fife or Gallatoun Pottery was founded in 1790 as a redware pottery, probably by William Mackie and William Grant. By May 1810, the partners were Robert Paterson and Andrew Gray, both potters, though Andrew Gray's brother Archibald appears also to have been a partner. In 1811 Paterson disappeared and one James Smith takes his place. By this time the pottery was making creamware and when Smith left in 1812 the Grays continued.

In 1817 a new pottery was built but in 1826 a general depression in trade led to Andrew Gray, sole surviving partner, being declared bankrupt. The Pottery was sold off along with its flint mill in the nearby town of Leven and was bought by John Methven, son of David Methven who owned the Links Pottery at the other end of Kirkcaldy. On John's death in 1837, the Works passed to his daughter and son-in-law, Mary and Robert Heron, and eventually to their son Robert Methven Heron.

In 1882 the pottery initiated a series of single-coloured pots, said to be based on the antique and called Wemyss Ware. Very shortly thereafter R.M. Heron brought back from his travels a number of East European earthenware painters to work for him. Most of them returned home soon after arriving but one, Karel Nekola, stayed on and trained native Scots in painting ceramics. From then on Wemyss Ware was painted on a white body and carried the pottery through till 1928. R.M. Heron died in 1906: Karel Nekola in 1915 but Wemyss Ware continued to be made till the pottery closed.

No wares are known with certainty from the earliest periods of Fife Pottery except for two pearlware plaques with a moulded bust of King George IIII marked Fife Pottery in Glasgow Museums. Until the advent of Wemyss Ware, Fife Pottery made the usual run of transfer-printed and painted wares along with coloured and sponge-printed pieces. Particularly interesting was a rather crude imitation of Bell's pattern Tamerlaine with an identical border but different central themes (20.5). These were all of fairly good quality but rather undistinguished.

However, the invention of Wemyss Ware raised the pottery to a new level. Wemyss Ware is fragile since it was fired at a low temperature to keep it white and absorbent. As well as this, the glaze has a distinct tendency to crackle. But the very high quality of the painting has made it a favourite with collectors in spite of these drawbacks. It is so popular that various attempts have been made in England and in Scotland to revive the ware and to claim a monopoly on the name but none has equaled the quality of the decoration on the original.

Many subjects appear on the pots: flowers (especially roses), fruit, birds, cockerels, insects, figure subjects, landscapes. There are even a few pieces with transfer prints of popular tourist spots. Around the turn of the twentieth century the pottery introduced a variant known as Earlshall Wemyss. This has a series of designs with trees, rooks, sundials, topiary and peacocks amongst other things.

Rosslyn Ware was made with red clay and a jet glaze with gold decoration for teapots and the pieces that go with them. Langtoun Ware was a rather jazzy successor to Wemyss in the final years of the pottery's working life.

Pottery Descriptions: Fife Pottery — incised
R.H. — printed
H. printed
R.Heron F.P.K. — printed
A heron on a shield — printed — a real mark
Wemyss Ware — impressed or written
R.H. & S.
T.Goode & Co. — a London retailer.

Reading: Anon. *The Kirkcaldy Potteries* — an exhibition catalogue. Kirkcaldy 1974
Davis, Peter and Rankine, Robert. *Wemyss Ware* Edinburgh & London: Scottish Academic Press, 1986.
Kelly, H.E. "An Imitative Pattern Attributed" in *SPHR* 11 (1987)
McNeill, Carol. *Kirkcaldy Potteries* — Kirkcaldy 1998: 57-59.
Quail, G. "The Fife or Gallatown Pottery" in *SPHR* 8 (1984): 14-19.

20.2. Mark on pitcher appearing in 20.1.

20.1. Pitcher with cream colored slip and moulded swans. 9" ht. (£35/$60).

Center left: 20.3. Serving dish: Willow. Pitchers: 1863 royal wedding and Fragaria. (£50/$150).

Center right: 20.4. Plate: Temple. Pitchers: painted outwith Pottery and printed with girl and lamb (reverse has Good Dash). (£40-50/$70-85).

Bottom left: 20.5. Fife's imitation of Bells' Tamerlaine, not marked or named. The border is an exact replica of Bells'. Punch bowl. Pitcher. Bowl. Teaplate. (£30-40/$50-70).

Bottom right: 20.6. Plates: Milan. This is Fife's standard lacustrine landscape. Pitcher with inscription, now badly worn. (£45/$75)

20.7. Wemyss Ware. Large vase painted by Karel Nekola, 20.5″ ht. (£10,000/$16,700).

20.8. Dog, 17.75" lgth. and vase, 15.25" ht. The dog blank may have been bought in (purchased from another company). Dog (£20,000/ $33,400). Vase (£2000/$3,400).

20.9. Pig, 18" lgth. (£3000/$5,000) and vases, 5" ht. (£200/$335).

20.10. Large Pig, 18" lgth. (£3000/$5,000). Small Pig, 6.5"lgth. (£300/$500). Cat, 12.50" ht. (£5000/$8,350).

20.12. Mark on the mug in 20.11.

20.11. Extremely rare transfer-printed mug, 3.75″ diam., 3.75″ ht. (£500/$850).

Center left: 20.13. Geese, 7″ - 8.25″ ht. (£300/$500). and trays, 10″ lgth. (£500-1500/$835-$2,500).

Center right: 20.14. Trays, 10″ lgth. (£500-1500/$835-2500).

Bottom left & right: 20.15 & 16. Round "Gordon" plates, 8″ diam. (£250-800/$385-1340).

20.17. Teapots, 3" - 6" ht. (£250-900/$420-1500).

20.18. Mugs, 4.50" diam., 5.75" ht. (£300-1500/$500-2500).

20.19. "Tygs" Loving cups, 9.50 diam., 9.5 ht., 8" diam., 7.75" ht. (£800-3000/$1340-5000).

20.20. Black background Wemyss. Tazza, 9.50" diam. (£1000/$1570). Pomade, 3.75" diam. (£500/$835). Pin Tray, 5.25" lgth. (£300/$500).

20.21. Baskets, 8", 12", 15.50" (£600-1500/$1000-2500).

20.22. Hat pin holders, 6" ht. (£300-800/$500-1340).

20.23. Stemmed bowl, 4.50" diam. and small pieces pot, 3.50" ht., 2" diam., jam pot (lidded), 4.75" ht. (£80/$135), punchbowl, 9" diam., 6.50" ht. (£100/$170)

20.24. Mugs and vase. (£300-800/$500-1340).

20.25. "Japan" vases, 13" ht., 15.25" ht. (£500, 10, 420/$835, 16, 700).

20.26. "Bute Vase," 11.50" ht., 6.25" diam. (£850/$1420).

20.27. A corner cupboard: ewer, 6.25" ht. & basin, 11" diam. (£1500/$2500), jug, 4.25" ht, cup, 3" diam., saucer, 4.75" diam., beaker vase, 4.25" ht., "Duchess" candlestick, 6.50" diam. (£250-800/$420-1340).

20.28. A bedroom set: chamber pot, 9.75" diam., spongeholder, 8.50" diam., vase, 8" ht., and pomade, 3.25" & 3.75" diam. (£500-1500/$835-2500).

20.30. Vases and dishes. Top shelf: Gypsy pots, 5" diam., 5" ht, ink wells, 8.50" lg. Bottom shelf: vases, 9" ht. & 5" ht. (£350-500/$580-2500).

20.29. Slop bucket, 11.50" diam. (£1500/$2500).

20.31. Plant stand (by Methven), 12" ht., bowl, 11" diam., 7.50" ht., and wall plaque, 17.25" lgth. Stand (£350/$580). Pot (£1500/$2500). Tray (£850/$1420).

20.32. Wall basket, 15″ wdth. (£850/$1420).
Heart tray, 12″ ht. (£1500/$2500).

20.33. Platter, 12″ lgth. (£750/$1260) and letter rack, 8.75″ lgth., 7″ ht. (£1500/$2500).

20.34. Earlshall Wemyss Jugs, 4.75″ ht., 7″ ht. (£300-600/$500-1000).

20.35. Langtoun Ware — children's tea set. (£150/$250).

20.36. Rosslyn Ware — tea kettle, creamer, sugar basin and lidded pitcher. (£25-40/$40-67).

20.37. Rosslyn Ware — sugar basin and pitchers. (£25-40/$40-67).

21

The Glasgow Pottery of John and Matthew Perston Bell & Co., Glasgow

In the Glasgow of 1841 two brothers from a merchant family — John and Matthew Perston Bell — pooled resources to found a pottery — officially the Glasgow Pottery but known throughout its life as "Bells". John, the more active partner and elder brother was a lawyer (known in Scotland as a 'writer'); Matthew was a shawl manufacturer and all his life had poor health.

The long-term reason for the brothers' decision to enter the pottery trade is not known but the precipitating factor was certainly the failure of the Anderston Pottery and the consequent availability of Robert Clough, its manager, a Yorkshire potter who had come to Glasgow some 20 years before. The Pottery was built beside a branch of the Forth and Clyde Canal and was in production by February 1842 with amazing speed. At first, general white earthenware with transfer-prints only was made but by 1847 china and parianware had been added to the repertoire. In 1860 the premises were greatly extended and the Glasgow Pottery had become the most important pottery in the history of the Scottish industry, both for the range and the quality of its wares. Its painted tea sets became the standard wedding china of the western Scottish middle class and its showroom one of the sights of Victorian and Edwardian Glasgow.

All classes of whiteware were made and every form of decoration was used. Transfer prints, hand painting, sponge-printing, mocha, slip banding, sprigging, etc. were used on china and earthenware of high quality. Even sanitary ware was made and hotels and shipping were supplied with thick, strong, white earthenware.

The export trade was not neglected and John Bell even became a shipowner to assist in this. Wares were sent to Ireland, Europe, North and South America, Africa, and—in the latter part of the nineteenth century—the area including India, Burma, Sri Lanka, Malaysia and Indonesia was flooded with specially designed transfer-printed ware and even high quality ware painted and sponge-printed in special patterns.

Matthew Bell died in 1871 and John in 1880 but the Pottery was, immediately after this, opened under the former manager James Murdoch as J. & M.P.Bell & Co. Ld. and was equally successful. However, several compulsory purchases of parts of the Pottery by railway companies and a general depression in trade caused the Pottery to close in 1912. Part of the site was used as a china warehouse by ex-employees for a few more years.

There is little doubt that the Glasgow Pottery was initially intended to manufacture goods for export since it was founded on such a large scale at a time of great depression in trade. There has consequently been a scarcity of its earliest products found in Scotland and some doubt as to their nature. Some very grand pieces were known from a gift made to Paisley Museum by Joseph Turner who was the Company's last Secretary. But these were obviously meant for display at the 1851 and 1862 Exhibitions in London. Everyday, commercially viable wares were scarcely represented in the donation.

In 1997, however, the site of the original Pottery lay empty and a limited excavation was carried out by Glasgow University Archaeological Research Division (GUARD) and Keith Speller, the archeologist, has published two interim reports.

This excavation, which found a large deposit of sherds datable to 1857 and before that, has extended our knowledge of Bells' early products greatly.

There was a great deal of china represented in the deposit, mainly in the form of teaware. Some of the soft paste porcelain had violet sprigs, seven sprigs in all being present. Several hexagonal pitchers with these sprigs have since been identified (21.1), some with white sprigs on drab. Parian ware was also present in the deposit, principally as pitchers and in shapes that were already known (21.2) but not attributed to so early a date before. Much white ironstone was found, some with moulded calla lilies, still unrecorded in Britain. But some sherds of a pitcher with mouldings of a variant of Ceres were present which was already known as both pitchers and pickle dishes (21.3). Spongeware was there in some quantity in the form of porringers only. The motifs were, as one would expect from this early date, rather underdeveloped and consisted mainly of concentric circles in blue or green.

Hexagonal pitchers are known apart from the dig in large numbers. Of the patterns, Jenny Lind is a commemorative for the opera singer's visit to Scotland, California of the Gold Rush, whereas Marine is the usual lacustrine landscape in flow blue or mulberry (21.4). Bohemia is another such, found on pitchers, wall plaques and bedroom sets, etc. (21.5). Hawking in the Olden Time (on pitchers), Hawking and Sporting Subjects (both on dinner ware) are all similar subjects (21.6). Bells' greatest success came with Triumphal Car, a changing pattern which began about 1860 and continued certainly till 1900 in many colors and forms (21.7). According to Fleming, this pattern was designed by David Roberts, the landscape artist of exotic scenes but this seems innately unlikely since Roberts was too successful at this date for pottery designing. Almost as successful as Triumphal Car was Italian Lakes, another changing pattern which began earlier than Triumphal Car but was rather overwhelmed by the latter's total success (21.8). Warwick Vase was never so successful but merits mention since Bells also made a replica of the Warwick Vase in parian and the original Vase has come to rest in the Burrell Collection in Glasgow. Recently found in South Africa were a cup and saucer of Corinth, a pattern which also features the Warwick Vase.

Porringer patterns include Swiss Subjects, Balmoral (21.9), and Reindeer (21.10). Tea ware has Gondola and Deer Stalking in earthenware (21.10). Invalid ware had toast-water pots with Triumphal Car and Marble and spit pots had Kew Gardens (21.11). Bedroom sets often had a moulded motif of the head of Medusa and snakes (21.12). These sets were sometimes almost completely undecorated but for exhibitions were elaborately painted and, since they have been seen painted in imitation of Nautilus Porcelain, the life of the shape must have been long.

Other shapes of pitcher in parian include Vintage, which was such a success that it was made in blue body also and in white earthenware. The range of sizes in parian leads one to suspect that at first Bells had difficulty in controlling this aspect of their parian (21.13).

Around 1857 a new pitcher shape was introduced which was to prove immensely popular. At first it was made with no decoration or only a little gold but quickly after this it appeared with many transfers on it (21.14). Sappho, Jeddo, British and Foreign Birds, Royal Conservatory, and Vine Border are amongst the patterns (21.14-16). Commemoratives include Burns (for a centenary) and Garibaldi (for a visit to Britain) (21.15, 17). The Wedding of the Prince of Wales to Princess Alexandra in 1863 produced wares for every size of purse: a parian pitcher, a transfer printed one, a moulded earthenware pitcher and a teaplate for the humblest (21.18). The Marble pattern, not actually given a name until after 1880, continued in both mulberry and green (21.32). Gothic Border is one of a number of pitcher patterns with a line of decoration around the belly. Painted pitchers in flow blue covered in pink lustre were common. Water Lily occurs on a less popular shape (21.33).

Dinner wares include mulberry patterns — Japan, Kensington, Anemone (21.29) — and blue — Harvest Scene, Harvest, Sardinia (21.20). The first was also used for punch bowls and was revived for wall plaques around 1905. Japan is also found in flow blue. Broseley and Willow were made in abundance and both were found on the dig (21.28). Neither name is ever found marked on wares until well into the twentieth century. Fibre and Apsley Plants were also made pre-1857 and found in the dig (21.29). Paraguay was perhaps meant for export (21.27). Palestine was a rather popular changing pattern with scenes from the Holy Land (21.30). May Morn is found only on bedroom ware (21.30). Victoria Scroll is another popular mulberry pattern (21.32). All this time it must be remembered mocha ware and other commercial slipwares were being produced but never marked (21.34). The usual kitchen ware, such as jelly moulds, were usually marked (21.35).

As the 1870s approached, a new parian pattern was made with strings of cameo shapes moulded on it. Identical pieces were made by Dudson of Staffordshire so the attribution of unmarked specimens should be done with caution (21.36). Similarly moulded teapots are found and moulded earthenware pitchers were made about this time (21.37). In fact all shapes and patterns were changed to suit changing tastes. Later tea ware decoration got more and more elaborate (21.31).

For the 1870s also new pitcher shapes were introduced, one of which was extremely elegant and popular. It appears with a great number of transfer prints such as Indian Cress and on a commemorative for the 1871 wedding of the Marquis of Lorne to Princess Louise, daughter of Queen Victoria. Figures representing the months were copied by Bo'ness (21.38-40). Dinner ware patterns became in general more abstract and restrained. Gone are lacustrine landscapes; 'Japanese' patterns like Corea are the rage and often appear in fashionable grey (21.42). Venetian was very successful but Tamerlaine became an international best seller, made by potteries also in Holland, France and Germany as well as in Glasgow (21.44). But more austere patterns became the norm, like Ivy Wreath and Denmark (21.45). At this time and hereafter, many plates were produced to private order, often for commercial businesses or church bazaars (21.46). The same changes happened to porringers, patterns like Ching giving way to Florence and patterns with insects (21.47). Chamber pots are commonly found from this period on (21.48) and cheese dishes, the latter often being marked GRANITE (21.49).

As 1880 approached, more changes were made. New cup shapes (21.50), new parian pitchers (21.51) and earthenware ones (21.52), some of which had colored transfers at this remarkably early date. Vases were made both in china and in granite and the latter body was used also for teapots and tea kettles (21.53-55). Spongeware and painted ware were made for home and overseas markets (21.56).

In the late 1870s, the 'Japanese' pattern was challenged by a new type of pattern. Patterns like Mikado and Arcadia (21.57) were displaced by abstract border patterns. The motifs were based usually on plants like Glenshee (21.58) but others have elements of landscape like Gouda (21.59). Sometimes the decoration descends almost to the centre of the plate as in Lorraine or Braemar (21.60), others are confined within borders like Bracelet and Louise (21.61, 62).

Similar changes were made to porcelain tea wares (21.63, 64, 65). At this time also Bells' tea cups were sometimes found painted outwith the pottery (painted by a source outside the pottery) by non-potters (21.66).

With the advent of J. & M.P. Bell & Co. Ld., many more changes were made. Foreign competition had reached the level where Dutch, German and Czech potteries were selling at less than cost. All British potteries had to respond to this and Bells did so in several ways.

Earthenware pitchers were produced in new shapes and patterns (21.68-72), some even being painted to resemble the new and popular Nautilus Porcelain. Commemoratives were made as well as figurines, illustrating best-selling books (21.74, 75). Wall plaques were elaborately hand-painted or printed and a great many in the 1880s were sold blank to be painted by others (21.77-80). 'Wally dugs' (earthenware dogs) were made as chimney piece decorations (21.81). Granite ware continued (21.82) and flow blue of the peculiarly Scottish kind was made, marked with a stamped saltire later used also by Methven of Kirkcaldy (21.83-4).

But the greatest innovation was a series of soup plates and rice dishes with specially designed patterns which were exported in enormous quantities to south-east Asia and elaborately sponge-printed and painted dishes for the same market. These have been found in India, Sri Lanka, Burma, Malaysia, Indonesia, Singapore and Sarawak (21.85-90). Our understanding of these has depended on pieces brought back from Java, Sarawak and Sri Lanka by several collectors.

Even with such success, Bells were in trouble at home when, in the first years of the twentieth century, the Caledonian Railway compulsorily bought a large piece of the west end of the pottery. The Company now had to buy in china from Aynsley of Staffordshire and remark it (21.91). The Works carried on until 1912 but at that point the Board decided to put the Company into liquidation and no wares have been identified later than this date (21.92).

The name was kept alive for a few years by the two former employees who rented part of the site as a china warehouse, but by 1930 even that had gone.

Pottery Descriptions:

Before 1881 J. & M.P.B. & Co — printed or impressed or as a padmark
J. & M.P.Bell & Co. — printed or impressed
JB in a bell impressed
After 1881 J. & M.P.B. & Co.Ld. transfer printed
B in a bell impressed or sponge-printed

Reading: Kelly, H.E. "The Parian Jugs of the Glasgow Pottery" and "The Earthenware Jugs of the Glasgow Pottery" both in *SPHR* 13 (1989): 13-29; 78-108.

______. "The 1844 Explosion in the Glasgow Pottery" in *SPHR*14 (1990): 6-10.

______. "John Bell's Marriage" (1855) in *SPHR*15 (1993): 37-99.

______. "The Export Trade of J. & M.P.Bell & Co. and other Scottish Potteries" and "Matthew Perston Bell's Will" both in *SPHR* 16 (1994): 49-57 & 58-61.

______. "The Story of J. & M.P.Bell & Co. Glasgow Pottery" in *SPHR* 18 (1996): 4-5.

______. "The Glasgow Pottery of John and Matthew Perston Bell" in *Scottish Industrial History* 16 (1993): 9-20.

______. The Glasgow Pottery of John and Matthew Perston Bell — to appear as a book.

Speller, Keith. "Bell's Pottery Glasgow" in *SPHR* 18 (1996)

______. "Bell's Pottery Glasgow" Interim report, Glasgow University Archaeology Research Dept. 325.2 (1996).

______. "Bell's Pottery Glasgow by Keith Speller." *GUARD* 325.4 (1996)

Pattern List:

This is divided into two: before and after 1880 when John Bell died. As usual, patterns which are illustrated are not described.

a) 1841-1880.

Achilles — pitcher with classical oval on each side.
Aden

Agra — exactly the same as the pattern made by Britannia.
Alhambra — returned from Java.
Amazon — lacustrine landscape with statue of an Amazon.
Amboina — returned from Java.
Anemone
Apsley Plants
Asiatic Pheasants — the usual pattern.
Athens — Greek vases on a plinth.
Aurora — an angel carrying a child.
Balmoral
Batavia
Bavaria — a trellis pattern.
Bohemia
Bracelet
Bramble — birds on bramble branches.
Brazil — banana plant and bird.
British and Foreign Birds
Broseley — never named on ware.
Burns — there are three Burns patterns, this is Burns I.
Butterfly — punch bowls with butterflies on amber panels.
California
Chinese Sports — two children fishing.
Ching — never carrying Bells' mark.
Chusan — returned from Java.
Copenhagen
Corea
Corinth — Greek key with the Warwick Vase.
Dagmar — a leafy border.
Damascus — same as Verreville pattern — returned from Java.
Deer Stalking
Delhi — returned from Java.
Denmark
Egyptian Vases — vase with scroll and flowers.
English Lakes — lacustrine landscape.
Falconry — mug illustrated in SPHR 8.
Fibre
Florence
Fokien — oval with oriental figures in a landscape.
Foreign Birds — two parrots — not to be confused with British & Foreign Birds.
Fungus — exactly the same pattern as Mushroom except for color.
Garibaldi
The Gem — border and centre both abstract.
German Stag Hunt — a hunting scene, the same as the Methven pattern of the same name.
Giraffe — two giraffes eating from a palm tree.
Glasgow — returned from Java.
Goatherds — scene with herds.
Going to Market
Golden Flower — floral
Gondola
Gothic Border
Grecian — anthemions often in two colors.
Grecian Border — Greek key round the belly of pitcher.
Griffen — griffens.
Harvest
Harvest Scene
Hawking
Hawking in the Olden Time
Herculaneum — classical battle scene with Amazons.
Holly Wreath — band of holly at edge and centre.
Humming Bird — returned from Java — humming bird.
Indian Cress
Indian Sprig — overall mulberry pattern of sprigs.
Indian Tree — exotic tree in an oval.
Ionia — putti.
Italian Lakes
Italy
Ivy Wreath
Japan
Japanese — a 'Japanese' pattern.
Jeddo
Jenny Lind
Kensington
Kew Gardens
Laurel — abstract border.
Lily and Rose — floral.
Loo Choo
(Lorne) — name often given to the pitcher commemorating the 1871 wedding but not by Bells.
Louise
Malacca — export pattern.
Malaga — Spanish scene
Maltese — elaborate Maltese crosses.
Marine
May Morn
Morning and Even — angel with child.
Mushroom — see Fungus.
Neuilly — lacustrine landscape.
Ning-po
Ophelia
Oriental — lacustrine landscape.
Palestine
Paraguay
Parisian Sprig — floral groups.
Pearl Border — row of abstract decoration on belly of ware.
Pekin
Persian
Pompeii — putto in chariot.
Primrose
Reindeer
Royal Conservatory
Royal Palace — urn full of roses in a room.
Rural — two girls in country setting.
Sappho
Sardinia — rustic landscape.
Scott
Sexagon
Siam — returned from Java.
Singapore — returned from Java
Spanish Goats — goats in a landscape.
Sporting Subjects
Stray Leaves
Swallow
Swiss Scenery
Swiss Subjects
Swiss Water Mill
Tamerlaine
Triumphal Car
Trojan — band of Greek key.
Vases — on a valve closet basin.

Venetian
Victoria Regia — lily pattern
Victoria Scroll
Vine Border
Vintage
Warwick Vase
Water Lily
Wellington — bust of Duke
Wild rose — usual pattern.
Willow
Woosung — returned from Java.
Yachting.

b) 1881-1912

Abergeldie — plant abstract
Aboyne — plant abstract.
Antoinette
Arcadia
Auburn — actually made by Aynsley, re-marked by Bells — floral.
Autumn — putti.
Ayam Jantam — cockerel — an export pattern.
Ballater — plant abstract.
Banda — export pattern.
Bangkok — dragon head with peacocks and flowers — export pattern.
Bird's Nest — nest among reeds.
Blythswood — a 'Japanese' pattern with central chrysanthemum.
Borneo — export pattern.
Bracelet
Braemar
Buah and Nanas
Buah Buah
Burmania — grotesque face and fruit.
Burns II
Burns III
Burong Metak — a peacock — export pattern
Burong Supan — dainty bird — export pattern.
Burung Kupu — birds and butterflies.
Cadzow
Cameo — panel with seated spinster.
Canova
Celebes
Chanon — dragon pattern.
Chantilley — plant pattern.
Clematis — floral overall pattern.
Clifton — plant abstract.
Coburg — wispy plant pattern.
Darnley — plant abstract.
Deeside — plant abstract.
Derby
Dragon — a coiled dragon — export pattern.
Drumlanrig — plant abstract
Dunblane — plant abstract.
Durian and Nanus — durian and pineapple — an export pattern.
Empress
Erchie
Eviction — scene with dogs.
Fantasia — bird, horseshoe, daisy, ivy, passion flower etc.
Glasgow Exhibition 1901
Glenartney — plant abstract.
Glenshee
Gouda
Grecian — usual sponge-printed pattern.
Haarlem — 'Japanese' pattern with flowers and ships.
Ikan China
Invercauld — plant abstract.
Japanese — a 'Japanese' pattern with a fan.
Johore — export pattern.
Kalantan
Kapal Basar — a ship — export pattern.
Keelin Hong — export pattern.
Keelung — export pattern.
Kelvin Grove
Kembang Bintang — flower and star — export pattern.
Kilmeny — edge and centre floral pattern
Kwantung — vase of flowers on a table — export pattern
Linnet — espaliered shrub with birds.
Loch-na-gar — plant abstract.
Lorraine
Louise
Makassar
Mayflower
Mikado
Mossgiel — plant abstract named after Burns' farm near Mauchline.
Oban — floral pattern with lattice.
Ochil — plant abstract.
Old Dutch
Orleans — plant abstract with shells.
Peacock and Lilies — export pattern.
Pegu
Pekin
Pompeii — putto in chariot.
Rosalind
Rosebery
Sandhurst — plant abstract.
Sarawak — export pattern
Sexagon
Seymour — plant abstract.
Singapore — floral pattern at rim and centre.
Stork — scene with stork
Strathearn — twigged branches with flowers.
Sumatra — export pattern.
Summer — roundels of flowers and prunus blossom
Sybil — plant abstract.
Tamerlaine
Tarlalu Bagus — export pattern.
Tokio — slanting stripes with flowers forming a deep border.
Triumphal Car
Tullibardine — plant abstract in Art Nouveau style.
Warwick — plant pattern
Watteau — plant abstract.
Yarrow — sparse floral pattern over peach coloured ground.

21.3. Export wares: white ironstone pitcher in a variant of the universal Ceres, 6.75" ht. (£120/$200) — a much later Copenhagen pitcher, c. 1875, 8.25" ht. (£120/$200) — and a plate with Batavia, c. 1870, 10.25" diam. (£50/$85).

21.1. Two pitchers with sprigs matching those from the dig. Left: white on drab — right: blue on white soft paste porcelain — both 7.50" ht. (£90/$150).

21.2. Two parian pitchers dated from shards found in a dig to pre-1857 — 7" & 8.25" ht. (£40, 120/$70, 200). The blue example is a Clyde Pottery imitation in earthenware, 8.50" ht. (£100/$170).

21.4. Three hexagonal pitchers: California, Marine, Jenny Lind, 7.75" ht. (£200, 100, 220/$340, 170, 370).

21.5. Bohemia as pitcher, 7.75" ht.(£100/$170), ewer and basin, 13" ht. (£160/$270), porringer, 7" diam. (£35/$60) and wall plaque, 8" diam. (£65/$110).

21.6. Hunting themes: Sporting Subjects, Hawking in the Olden Time, Hawking. Plates: 10.50" diam. (£35/$60). Pitcher: 5.75" ht. (£40/$70).

21.7. Triumphal Car in various colors and uses. Platters: 20" & 15" lgth. (£180/$300). Ewer: 10.75" ht. (£70/$120). Underdish: 8.75" diam. (£35/$60). Bowl: 7" diam. (£40/$70). Cup and saucer: 5.75" diam. (£ 50/$85). Toothbrush holder: (£30/$50).

21.8. Italian Lakes in various colors and uses. Platter:15" lgth. (£160/$270). Plate: 10.25" diam. (£35/$60). Underdish: 8.75" diam. (£35/$60). Tureen: 14" lgth. (£100/$170).

21.9. Porringers: Swiss Subjects, Balmoral, 7" diam. (£35/$60). Plate: Warwick Vase, 9.50" diam. (£35/$60).

21.10. Porringer: Reindeer, 7.75" diam. (£36/$60). Cups & saucers: Gondola, Deer Stalking, 5.75" diam. (£50/$85 each).

21.11. Invalid ware: toast water pots with Marble, 8.50" ht. (£60/$100) and Triumphal Car, 7.25" ht. (£50/$85). Spit pot with Kew Gardens, 5" diam. (£40/$70).

21.12. Ewer and basin with Medusa's head and snakes, 18.25" ht. (£280/$470).

21.13. Vintage — parian pitchers and earthenware versions, 7.75" - 10.75" ht. (£60-80/$100-135).

21.14. Pitchers: Sappho, white slip, Jeddo after 1857, 8.75" ht. (£60/$100).

21.15. British & Foreign Birds, Royal Conservatory, Burns I, 7.75" ht. (£60-100 [Burns]/$100-170).

21.16. Bread plate, 9.50" (£40/$70) and porringer: Loo Choo, 6.75" diam. (£35/$60). Pitcher: Vine Border, 7.75" ht. (£60/$100). Plate: Swiss Water Mill, 10.25" diam. (£60/$100).

21.17. Pitchers: Garibaldi from c. 1871, 8.25" ht. and c. 1861, 8.75" ht. (£100/$170).

21.18. Royal Wedding of 1863 - souvenirs pitchers: 8", 8.75", 8.25" (£90-150/ $150-250). Plate: 7" diam. (£50/$85).

21.19. Mulberry patterns. Plates: Kensington, Anemone, 10.50" diam. (£40/$70). Platter: Japan, 19.75" (£180/$300). Porringer: Ning-po, 7" diam. (£35/$60).

21.21. Typical garter mark of the 1870s.

21.20. Plates: Going to Market, Harvest, 10.50" diam. (£40/$70). Wall plaque (c. 1905) and punch bowl: Harvest Scene, 10" diam. (£70/$120).

21.22. Porcelain teawares: basic colors. Teaplates: 7.25" (£70/$120).

21.23. Porcelain teawares: painted tea set (1870s). Half tea set (six places) (£500/$835).

21.24. Porcelain dessert service: painted landscapes (1870s). Twelve places, etc. (£500/$835).

21.25. Porcelain dessert service: botanical illustrations (1870s). Twelve places etc. (£1000/$1700).

21.26. Moulded earthenware dessert service. (1860s or 1870s). Twelve places (£275/$460).

21.27. Platter: Paraguay, 12.75" lgth. (£90/$150).

21.28. Willow and Broseley. Platter, 12.75" lgth. Plates, 10.50" diam. Serving dish, 10.50". (£20-30/$35-50).

21.29. Patterns found in a dig date from before 1857: Broseley, Fibre, Apsley Plants. Platter, 15" lgth. (£65/$110). Cup and saucer: 3.25" cup diam. (£30/$50). Trio (£40/$70).

21.30. Palestine, May Morn, Palestine. Plate: 10.50" diam. (£35/$60). Ewer: 13.50" ht. (£200/$340). Platter: 13" lgth. (£60/$100).

21.31. Later tea ware — 1870s and 1880s. Trio (£70/$120). Single cups (£30/$50).

21.32. Pitchers: Marble in mulberry and green, 8.75" ht. (£50/$85). Underplate: Victoria Scroll, 12.75" diam. (£50/$85).

21.33. Gothic Border, painted, Water Lily, 8.75" & 8.25" ht. (£60-80/ $100-135).

21.34. These pieces may or may not be by Bells but they are similar to wares which were made at the Glasgow Pottery from 1841 at least until 1880, as well as by many other potteries. They were never marked. (£20-65/$35-100).

21.35. Jelly moulds, 6.75" - 8.25" lgth. (£25-30/$40-50).

21.36. Parian ware from c. 1870, 3.75" & approx. 9" ht. (£45, 80/ $75, 135).

21.37. Moulded pitchers with fish wives and hunting scenes, 6.75" ht. (£40-100/$70-170).

21.38. Pitchers: Indian Cress, Pompeii, 8.25" ht. (£80/$135). Porringer: Persian - 1870s, 7.25" diam. (£35/$60).

21.39. Grecian, 1871 royal wedding, the months, Swallow — 1870s, 8.25" ht. (£60-140/$100-235).

21.40. Scott, Ophelia, Stray Leaves, 8.25" ht. (£60-140/$100-135).

21.41. Pitchers: Primrose, 8" & 7.75" ht. (£70/$120). Teaware: Jeddo: bread plate, 9.50" diam. (£30/$50), cup & saucer, 6.25" diam. (£35/$60).

21.42. Corea — 1870s. Serving dish & underdish, 14.50" lgth.; dinner set (twelve places) (£300/$500).

21.43. Venetian and Persian. Cheese dish, 13" (£200/$340). Plate, 10.50" diam. (£35/$60). Bowl, 7" diam. (£35/$60).

21.44. Tamerlaine — 1870s. Punch bowl, 10" diam. (£60/$100). Pitcher, 7.75" ht. (£40/$70). Bread plate, 9.50" diam. (£40/$70). Teaplate, 7.25" diam. (£34/$50).

21.45. Ivy Wreath, Denmark — 1870s. Plate, 10.50" (£30/$50). Platters, 11.50" and 15" (£50/$85)

21.46. Wares made as private commissions — 1870s and 1880s: 7.50" to 11" (£60-80/$100-135).

21.48. Porringer: Aden, 7.25" diam. (£35/$60). Chamber pot: Maltese, 9" diam. (£40/$70).

21.47. Porringers: Florence, Ching, pattern with insects, 7.75" diam. (£35/$60 each).

21.49. Granite ware cheese dishes (£120/$200).

21.50. Tea plate: 7" diam. (£30/$50). Breakfast cup, 3.75" diam. (£25/$40), Tamerlaine cup, 3" diam. (£20/$35), cup with Christmas roses, approx. 6" diam. (£60/$100).

21.51. Later parian pitchers — 1870s and 1880s. Dandelion, 8.75" ht., Celtic, 9.25" ht., unlidded basketry, 8.50" ht., lidded basketry, 9.75" ht. (£40-70/$70-120).

21.52. Pitchers: coloured transfer, Yachting, Italy — c. 1875, 7.75" ht. (£100/$170 each).

21.53. Vases: Granite ware, 8.75" & 11.75" ht. and porcelain, 9.75" ht., the last with a painted landscape (£25-70/$40-120).

21.54. Granite ware teapot, 8.50" lgth. (£60/$100).

21.55. Granite ware tea kettle — hand painted, 7.50" ht. (£200/$340).

21.56. Back: painted plate with Persian Rose pattern, 9" diam. (£70/ $100). Front: Grecian, 8.75" diam. (£20/$35) and a rice dish, 9" diam., made for the Burmese market (£50/$85).

21.57. Mikado, approx. 6.50" lgth, Arcadia, 10" diam. — 1880s (£20/$35 each).

21.58. Glenshee: large plate, 9.25" diam., small plate, 7" diam. (£20/$35 each).

21.59. Gouda: serving dish, 12" lgth. Dinner service [twelve places] (£250/$425).

21.60. Serving dish: Lorraine, 11.75" lgth. (£35/$60). Sauceboat: Braemar, 6" lgth. (£25/$40).

21.61. Bracelet, approx. 9.50" lgth., Louise (brown), 13.75" lgth. (£20/$35) each.

21.62. Louise (blue) dinner plate, 10.75" diam. Dinner set [twelve places] (£250/$425).

21.63. Rosalind in porcelain. It is also known in an earthenware body. Plates, 7" diam. Tea set [six places] (£200/$340).

21.64. Porcelain teaware, mostly made by Aynsley. Teaplate, 7" diam. (£40/$70); saucers, 5.25' diam. Cup & saucer (£60/$100).

21.65. Porcelain teaware made by Bells. Bread plate, 9.75" diam. Tea set [six places] (£100/$170).

21.66. Bells' cup and saucers painted by a source outside the Pottery, probably by one of the Glasgow ladies — saucer, 5.75" diam. Cup & saucer (£90/$150).

21.67. Vases — 1880s — 13.75" ht. (£450/$750).

21.68. Pitchers: Cadzow, Old Dutch, Jeddo, 7.25" ht. (£60/$100).

21.69. Pitchers: Rosebery, Empress, 7.75" ht. (£70/$120).

21.70. Pitchers: Canova, painted, approx. 6" & approx. 7.25" ht. (£35/$60).

21.71. Pitchers: Victorina, Yarrow, painted imitation of Nautilus porcelain — 1890s. 5" - 9" ht. (£35-100/$60-170).

21.72. Pitchers: for New Year, Derby, Jeddo, 7.75" ht. (£70/$120).

21.73. Burns III — Punch bowl, approx. 10" diam. (£75/$125); pitchers, 7" & 8" ht. (£70-90/ $120-150).

21.74. Vase: Erchie, 3.25" ht. (£50/$85). Plates: Mayflower, 7" & 9.50" diam. (£20, 35/$35, 60).

21.75. Wee Macgreegor — this and Erchie are derived from best-selling books of the early twentieth century, approx. 6" ht. (£120/$200).

21.76. Pitcher: Kelvin Grove, 8" ht. (£200/$340).

21.77. Wall plaques, painted (r.) by an amateur, and (l.) probably in the Glasgow Pottery, 10" & 12.50" diam. (£50, 90/$85, 150).

21.78. Wall plaques: Burns II, classical landscape — 1900s — 10" diam. (£80/135 each).

21.79. Wall plaques: private commission (1905) and colored transfer — 9.50" diam. (£70/$120 each).

21.80. Wall plaque: Glasgow Exhibition 1901 — 10" diam. (£80/$135).

21.81. 'Wally dugs' - earthenware dogs, c. 1900, approx. 14" ht. (£350/$585 the pair).

21.82. Granite ware cheese dishes, 7.75" diam., 9.50" lgth. (£60/$100 each).

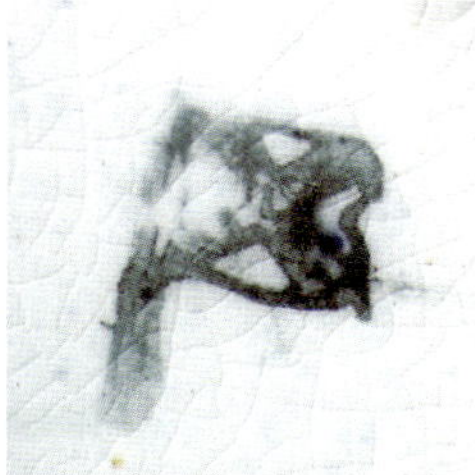

21.84. Mark on the flow blue depicted in image 21.83.

21.83. Flow blue plate and bowl, 9.75" & approx. 10.75" diam. (£45, 40/$75, 70)

21.85. Export transfers: Pegu x 3 and Kalantan, 9.50", 10.75" diam. (£70-80/$120-135).

21.86. Export transfers: Back — Burmania; front — Buah Buah and Pekin, 9.50" diam. (£70-80/$120-135).

21.87. Export transfers: Back — Celebes; front — Ikan Chira, Makassar, 9.50" diam. (£70-80/$120-135).

21.88. Export transfers: Buah and Nanas, Sexagon, 9.50" diam. (£70-80/$120-135).

21.89. Export transfer: unnamed, 9.50" diam. (£70-120).

21.90. Export spongeware — returned from India. Large bowl, 13.25" diam. (£160/$270). Rice dish, 10.75" diam. (£100/$170).

21.91. Export spongeware — returned from Sri Lanka — approx. 10.50" diam. (£100/$170).

21.92. Export spongeware — returned from Sri Lanka — approx. 11" diam. (£120/$200).

21.93. Commemorative plate for 1911 Coronation of George V and Queen Mary, perhaps the last order carried out by Bells. (£45/$75).

22

Govancroft Pottery, Glasgow

The only information in print about this Pottery is that it was founded about 1911 and the director was one James Buchanan.

It was situated at the extreme east end of Glasgow and until 1946 made nothing but utilitarian stonewares with a Bristol glaze. Whisky jars are still found in great numbers, sometimes with their basketry carriers still intact. In 1922 the pottery is described by one rival firm as having almost cornered the market in jam jars.

Before 1946, Govancroft's wares are the most ordinary of commercial and domestic stonewares. But between 1946 and 1976 the range of wares and the inventiveness are dazzling. Ordinary stoneware, particularly for the kitchen, continued to be made (22.1, 2), but a series of pitchers and baskets was designed, often with dabbed color under an opalescent glaze (22.3-5). Sometimes, instead, plain colors or dabbing were used under a fairly matt glaze (22.6-12). Flower baskets and oval bowls were particularly popular (22.5, 7-10).

In the fifties, coffee and tea sets with a limited range of granular colors under a matt glaze were introduced. Gray, oatmeal, mustard yellow and sage green were amongst the colors used (22.13). Similar dinner services followed (22.14). Towards the end of the fifties, various experiments were tried out with curdled glazes and translucent green glazes (22.15), amongst other things, but three lines were immediately successful.

(1) Inevitably a set of goods was produced based on thistles (22.17). Called Highland Ware, it is better designed than most of the dreary pieces produced for the tourist trade. (2) A range of small moulded animals was, and still is, immensely successful (22.18). (3) A set of spirit bottles moulded as books and given title such as Spirit of Scotland (whisky) and Spirit of Spain (sherry) have been found as far afield as New York flea markets.

In the sixties the market seems to have been much more competitive. Many ways to combat this were tried: dinner sets were painted (22.21), garden ornaments were made (22.22), but the most successful was the manufacture of whisky flagons with a very glassy glaze (22.21). The success of this was so great that it was a factor in the taking over of the pottery and its subsequent closure.

An interesting offshoot of Govancroft was Campsie Ware. In 1952 Edward Langley, a Liverpudlian who had worked until then with Govancroft, decided to set up a pottery on his own account. He used one gas-fired kiln at a site in central Glasgow and worked there for three years, making mainly slip-cast ornamental wares with a lustrous glaze.

After a fire in Govancroft Pottery, Langley was joined by five or six workers from the temporarily-closed Pottery and he moved in 1955 to Hillington, an industrial estate in south-west Glasgow. Here he had two electric kilns.

After 20 years at Hillington his lease was up and he moved one kiln to his farmhouse home north of Glasgow near the Campsie Hills. He died in 1982.

That Campsie Ware is strongly reminiscent of Govancroft's wares is not surprising but animals figure in the Campsie output much more than in Govancroft's, particularly birds. Besides Campsie Ware Langley made many small ornamental pieces for other potteries. These are either not marked or are marked as coming from the commissioning firm which makes them very difficult to identify.

Pottery Descriptions, both stamped and impressed: Govancroft Pottery
Govancroft
Campsie Ware — stamped

Reading: Cruickshank, G. *Campsie Ware* — Glasgow Public Libraries, 1992.

22.1. Early bottle in wicker basket, 11.50" ht. (£40/$70). Kitchen ware from various dates — storage jar, 4.50" ht. (£5-20/$8-35).

22.2. Hot water bottle and more kitchen ware (£5-25/$8-40).

22.3. Ornamental pitchers and bowls with dabbed color and opalescent glaze, 3.50" - 10" ht. (£10-50/$17-85).

22.4. Ornamental pitchers and bowls with dabbed color and opalescent glaze. Note the similarity of the taller pitcher to the one in photo 22.26. They were both moulded by Edward Langley. Bowl, 9" diam. (£40/$70); small bowl, 3.50" diam. (£30/$50); pitchers (£30-50/$50-85).

22.5. Shallow bowl, 10.75" diam. (£40/$70) and flower bowls, 9.50" - 10" lgth. (£30-40/$50-70).

22.6. Wares with a more matt glaze. Large pitcher, 9" ht., small creamer, 3.50" ht. Large pitcher (£50/$85); creamer (£5/$8).

22.7. Flower bowls, 7.50" - 15" lgth. (£15-25/$25-40).

22.8. Flower bowls, 7.50" - 15" ht. (£15-35/$25-60)

22.9. Flower bowls, 7.50" - 14" ht. (£15-35/$25-60) with vase, approx. 9" ht. (£30/$50).

22.10. Pitcher, approx. 7" ht. (£ 15/$25), jardiniere, approx. 14" lgth. (£20/$35) and flower bowl, approx. 14" lgth. (£30/$50).

22.11. Tea and coffee ware: teapot, 7.50" lgth. (£30/$50), small pitcher (rt.), 6" ht. (£15/$25), others (£15-25/$25-40).

22.12. Pitcher, 9.75" ht. (£40/$70), ash tray, approx. 6" diam. (£20/$35) and flower bowls, 4" - 10" lgth. (£15-35/$25-60).

22.13. Tea and coffee wares: pots, 8.50" and 10.50" ht. Coffee or tea set [6 places] (£60/$100).

22.14. Dinner and storage wares: plates, 10" diam., casserole, 9" diam., storage jars, 5.75"ht. (£5-30/$8-50)

22.15. Miscellaneous wares: ash tray, 4.50" diam., pitchers, 6.75" - 7.50" ht.(£5-30/$8-70).

22.16. Vase with curdled glaze, pitcher with translucent green glaze, two commissioned pieces, vases and ash tray: vase, 10" ht. (£30/S50), ash tray, 8" diam. (£30/$50), whisky flagon, 8.25" ht.(£25/$40), the rest (£10-30/$17-50).

22.17. Highland Ware and mug: large pitcher, 8" ht., creamer, 3" ht. (£5-25/$8-40)

22.18. Animals [squirrel, 4.25" ht.] (£25-50/$40-85) .

22.19. Spirit bottles. The complete set in either size would have eight books: large, 7.50" ht., small, 3.50" (£30/$50 - £15/$25 each).

22.20. Slip moulded mug with black glaze, approx. 4.50" ht. (£5/$8).

22.21. Dinner ware and whisky bottle with glassy glaze: plates, 8" - 10" diam. (£25/$40), whisky bottle, 7" ht. (£25/$40).

22.22. Garden ornaments and kitchen ware: 2" - 8" ht. (£2-15/$3-25).

22.23. Early stoneware mark.

22.24. Mark used in 1940s and 1950s.

22.25. Mark from garden ornament.

22.26. Campsie Ware: souvenir shell, 5.50" lgth. (£20/$35) and pitcher, 8.25" ht. (£25/$40).

22.27. Wares made by Langley for others: approx. 3.50" ht. (£5/$8 each).

22.28. Vase, 7" ht. (£15/$25), sugar and cream, 3.50" ht. (£15/$25), thistle salt and pepper, 2.50" ht. (£5/$8).

22.29. Campsie animals [stork 11" ht] (£20-50/$35-85).

23

Hydepark Pottery and Springburn Pottery, Glasgow

Hydepark Pottery requires a lot more investigation before its history can be definitively written. It was founded in 1837 by William McAdam in western Glasgow. Associated with William from time to time was his brother John, also a potter, but John's function in the duo is unclear. He has been described as partner and as manager. The first seems unlikely on the evidence. William also owned a glass bottle works next door to the Pottery. Hydepark made general stoneware, plumbago crucibles, and Rockingham-glazed teapots.

Fleming claims that the pottery was moved to the Gallowgate in eastern Glasgow but this is almost certainly wrong. Throughout the life of Hyde Park, William McAdam was involved in many financial transactions to the tune of thousands of pounds but glass and pottery were not his only business concerns. Sometime in the late 1870s the pottery and Glassworks were disposed of and a completely new and modern pottery was erected in Springburn in northern Glasgow. This Pottery was intended to make whiteware but the first kilns, drawn in 1879, were unsatisfactory. The ware was too heavy and not white enough.

William McAdam was at this time a member of a building syndicate which went bankrupt in the general depression of the late 1870s, following the bankruptcy of the City of Glasgow Bank and this together with the considerable outlay on his new Pottery brought about McAdam's own bankruptcy.

At first the Works could not be sold but the machinery was stripped out at the sale by other potteries. Eventually the buildings were bought by the Campbellfield Pottery Company.

William McAdam is said to have emigrated to New Zealand where he opened a small pottery in Dunedin and made teapots there until his death. His emigration has been denied by some writers but no real evidence was offered for this denial.

Remarkably few wares have been identified from this Pottery and those that have been are of the commonest kind of commercial stonewares. Nothing at all has been identified from McAdam's period at Springburn.

Pottery Descriptions: impressed

McAdam Hyde Park Pottery

Reading: Quail, G. "The Erroneous Wares Attributions in J.A.Fleming's 'Scottish Pottery'" in *SPHR* 11 (1984): 36-56.

24

Industrial and West Lothian Potteries, Bo'ness

The idea for the Scottish Wholesale Co-operative Society to erect its own pottery seems first to have been discussed in 1887. By March of the following year the town of Bo'ness on the banks of the river Forth had been chosen as the site. The presence of trained potters and coal in the area would have been a major factor in the decision.

It was not, however, until 1891 that construction was started. Meanwhile C.W. McNay had conceived, built and got into production the nearby Bridgeness Pottery. The Co-op's Company was known by many variations of a single name, e.g. the Bo'ness Industrial Co-operative Pottery and Manufacturing Society, Limited, but is usually referred to as the Industrial Pottery. Its capital was £7000.

By 1892 it was in production and the share capital had been increased by over £1400. But this had not been fully taken up by the public, nor had the pottery managed full production. By 1893 the pottery was running at a considerable loss. Efforts were made to shore the Company up by organising loans but these never materialised and in November 1893 the expedient was adopted of appointing a new manager. This totally failed to produce the result expected and in February 1894 the Company went into liquidation.

The same premises were subsequently occupied from 1896 until well into the twentieth century by the West Lothian Pottery Co. Ltd. of which little is known. Only one marked piece has ever been reported.

The Industrial Pottery seems only to have made fairly coarse white earthenware decorated with transfer prints or hand-painting. The wares are distinctly utilitarian and aimed towards the lower end of the market. Unmarked but certainly from the Industrial Pottery is a number of bread plates with gadroon mouldings and the central legend With the Compliments of the Season from ...... Co-op. Society Ltd. (24.2, 3). The blank is filled in with various names, all from the central belt of Scotland.

A problem with the unmarked wares is that the subsequent West Lothian Pottery Coy. Ltd. bought some of the moulds and transfer patterns, making their products frequently indistinguishable from those of the Industrial Pottery and perhaps even from McNay's (24.4-7). One pattern, Madge, has been published with a West Lothian mark but so far that is the only one (24.4).

Pottery Descriptions: all printed

Industrial Pottery, Bo'ness
Bo'ness Industrial Pottery & Manufacturing Society Ltd.
West Lothian Pottery Coy. Ltd.

Pattern List for Industrial Pottery:

Drill — scene with children
Phileau
Roseberry
Willow — the usual

Pattern List for West Lothian Pottery Co. Ltd.:

Madge

24.1. Willow plate, 10.50" diam. (£30/$50), painted cheese dish, 7.50" lgth. (£40/$70), and pitcher, 7.50" ht. (£35/$60).

24.2. Co-operative plate and plate with colored transfer, 10.25" diam. (£40/$70).

24.3. Two bread plates, 10.25" diam. and painted pitcher, 7.5" high. (£40/$70 each).

24.4. Three plates: Madge, General Sir Redvers H. Buller, and painted bird and nest, 10.25" diam. (£15-25/$25-40).

24.5. Transfer-printed plates, 10.25" diam. (£15-25/$25-40).

24.6. Ewer and basin with imitation marble pattern, approx. 12" ht. (£55/$90).

24.7. Mark on wares shown in photo 24.6.

25

The Links Pottery, Kirkcaldy

The Links Pottery, Kirkcaldy, known throughout its latter days as 'Methven's', was started as early as 1714 by William Adam, architect and father of the much more famous Robert, as a brick and tile work. In 1773 one David Methven became manager and three years later bought the works and clay rights for £400.

By 1805 redware was being made as well as bricks and in 1809 the premises were greatly extended to form both a brickwork and a pottery. In 1827 the property was divided between two brothers and John Methven continued to make redware and also bought the nearby Fife Pottery which made creamware.

In 1847 the pottery passed into the hands of David Methven and around this time the pottery began to make whiteware. In 1870 the partnership was between James Methven and A.R.Young who was the works' traveler. In 1892 A.R.Young and Sons became the sole proprietors and in 1897 a new Pottery was built. The Pottery closed in 1928.

Methven's employed in its heyday over 100 people and produced a range of transfer-printed earthenware which is rather derivative and undistinguished when it is not simply copied from other potteries. The reason for this is presumably that their main output was in painted wares, sponge-printed wares and those combining the two. This could be said to be a characteristic also of the Fife Pottery. Of all the Scottish potteries, the Links produced the most carefully made and clearly identifiable spongeware, even without taking into consideration the fact that they marked it more than any other pottery. Airlie Ware, Nisbet Ware and Auld Heather Ware are trade names for spongeware for special markets, the last being intended for North America but never having got there due to industrial action. This is quite a different attitude to spongeware from that adopted by most other potteries who aimed it at the cheapest markets and were almost ashamed of making it, in some cases to the extent of denial.

In the 1860s a number of pitchers was issued with transfer patterns on what was undoubtedly a Clyde Pottery pitcher shape. A possible explanation is that Links, under pressure of orders, bought blanks from Clyde and decorated them. Roman and Butterfly were amongst these (25.5).

Several Methven patterns were copies of some made by other potteries, e.g. Verreville's Damascus (25.2) and Clyde's British Rivers. Their own standard lacustrine landscape pattern was Verona which was extremely popular (25.1, 3, 14). In later years other, more original patterns were introduced such as Tom Tit for pitchers and Kent for teaware (25.7). Commemoratives were made for the Edinburgh Exhibition of 1886 and for Queen Victoria's Jubilee in 1887 (25.4, 9). Other popular prints were Cumae (25.2), Tudor (25.3), Berry (25.9) and Pomegranate (25.6). At least one Christmas pitcher was made (25.9).

In the 1880s, they introduced Abbotsford Ware in close imitation of Wemyss Ware. Self-colored and flower-painted pieces were made, the latter even painted at times by the same people who painted Wemyss Ware (25.15, 16).

But nothing in their output prepares one for the Links Pottery's export spongeware (25.24-28). Bells', Methven and the Société Cêramique of Maastricht all produced large rice dishes and soup plates for the Asian market. These are extremely well designed and executed, sometimes sponge-printed only, sometimes painted as well. The products of the three potteries are indistinguishable so it is impossible to tell who initiated and who copied these patterns. Obviously all three potteries kept an eye on each other. Included in this trade was Methven's version of Scottish flow blue (25.27, 28) where the blue is allowed to flow almost without control. All of this, however, was not enough to see the Pottery through the bad times in the 1920s. In spite of its two hundred years of fine manufacture, it closed in 1928.

Pottery Descriptions: David Methven & Sons
D.M. & Sons
D.M. & SS — all transfer-printed

Readings: Reid, Laura & Goulder, Margaret. *The Links Pottery, Kirkcaldy.* — Kirkcaldy Museum, 1984.

McNeill, Carol. *Kirkcaldy Potteries* — Kirkcaldy: Fife Publicity, 1998.

Pattern List :

Antique
Asiatic Pheasants
Beatrice
Berry
Blossom — floral
Bosphorus — the Bo'ness pattern.
Bramble
Brig O' Doon
British Rivers
Burgundy — doubtful
Butterfly
Caller Herrin — Caller Ou — Never marked but certainly Methven's.
Canova
Chili — tea ware and pitchers
China
Ching
Clarence
Classical Vases
Clyde
Coronation — Edward VII and Alexandra.
Crystal Palace
Cumae
Daffodil
Daisy
Damascus
Danish
Derby — tea ware
Edina — deep floral border
Fern — border pattern of ferns
Fibre
Fife
Flaxman — named in *Pottery Gazette* for August 1899.
Forth
Fountain
Garland — there seem to be two related patterns with this name.
German Stag Hunt — a hunt scene shared with Bells' Glasgow Pottery.
Grecian — both printed and sponge-printed forms of the usual pattern.
Imperial — classic border
International Exhibition Edinburgh 1886
Iona
Japan
Jay — bird amongst strawberries.
Jubilee
Kaiser
Kent
Lorne
Maltese
May
Milan
Montrose
Nightingale — two birds on a nest with four eggs
No.1000
Oban
Oriental — birds and trellis with foliage.
Osborne
Parrot
Pastoral — landscape with castle and cattle
Peace
Playmates
Pomegranate
Roman
Rose
Rose and Vine
Serapis — deer in a landscape
Spiral — so far seen only in U.S.A.
Squirrel
Stag — deer in a landscape
Sultan
Swallow
Teck
Tom Tit
Tudor
Tulip
Turkey
Unity
Verona
Victoria — sheet pattern of flowers
Views — an overall pattern of 'Japanese' type
Water Hemlock — the plant
Wild Rose — the usual pattern — brought back from Java.
Willow
Windsor — floral
York

25.1. Back: unnamed pattern and Verona. Front: Verona, 8" - 15" diam. (£25-60/$40-100).

25.2. Pitcher: Cumae. Ashet and plate: Damascus, 8" - 12" (£30-80/ $50-135).

25.3. Pitcher: Tudor, 8" ht. (£45/$75). Plate: Verona, 10" diam. (£25/$40).

25.4. Cheese dish and creamer for the 1886 Edinburgh Exhibition showing the Exhibition ground with a balloon hovering over it and various parts of the reproduction pieces of Old Edinburgh built for the Exhibition, 8.75" diam. (£175/$290).

25.5. Clyde shape pitchers with Butterfly and Roman, 8.75" ht. (£50/$85).

25.6. Punch bowl: Pomegranate, approx. 10" diam. (£80/$135).

25.7. Pitchers: Tom Tit and unnamed, approx. 8.50" ht. (£40-55/$70-90). Teaware: Kent, approx. 5.50" diam. (£45/$75).

25.8. Plate: Rose and Vine, 10.75" diam. (£30/$50). Pitcher: moulded and unnamed, 9" & 7.75" ht. (£50/$85).

25.9. Pitchers: Christmas, Berry and Jubilee, 8.25" ht. (£35-100/$60-170). Plate is unmarked but carries Jubilee pattern and is one of a pair, dated 1837 and 1887, 9.75" diam. (£55/$90 the pair).

25.10. Jubilee mark.

25.11. Porringer: unnamed, 7" diam. (£35/$60). Plate: No.1000, 9.25" diam. (£25/$40).

25.13. Mark on moulded pitcher in photo 25.8.

25.12. Plates: Asiatic Pheasant, sheet pattern, Canova, approx. 8" - approx. 9" diam. (£15-25/ $25-40).

25.14. Creamer: sponge-printed and painted, approx. 4" ht. (£45/ $75). Pitchers: Verona and unnamed, 7.50" - 8.75" ht. (£40/$70).

25.15. Abbotsford Ware: 7"-8" (£60-100/$100-170).

25.16. Two pieces of Abbotsford Ware, 4.50" ht. (£55-$90) and a long necked bottle with blue glaze and gold decoration, 12.75" ht. (£100/ $170).

25.17. Similar bottle decorated outside the Pottery, 12.75" ht. (£50/$85).

25.18-20. Assorted pieces of Airlie Ware, Nisbet Ware and Auld Heather Ware. They are indistinguishable (£35-150/$60-250).

25.21. Painted cheese dishes and typical spongeware (£35-120/$60-200).

25.22. Auld Heather Ware (£40-60/$70-100).

25.23. Typical spongeware (£40-100/$70-170).

25.24-25. Dishes returned from Sri Lanka, approx. 11" diam. (£120/$200).

25.26. Mark on wares returned from Sri Lanka.

25.27-28. Scottish flow blue piece and mark, returned from Sri Lanka, approx. 10" diam. (£70-120).

25.29. Bowl: Unity, 5.50" diam. (£30/$50). Plate: Pastoral, 9" diam. (£35/$60).

26

Midlothian Pottery, Portobello

This was founded as a redware pottery at an unknown date in the late eighteenth century by William Jamieson, an Edinburgh builder, probably to supply bricks and tiles for the building of Edinburgh's New Town in which he took a part. In 1790 he was advertising creamware but in 1796 the pottery was leased by Cookson & Jardine, china retailers, and by 1808 it was in the hands of Thomas Rathbone & Co. These Rathbones were connected to the English family who were well known in the Potteries. Thomas Rathbone died in 1826 but the pottery stayed in the hands of the Rathbone family until 1853 with a short break from 1839 to 1844 when it was known as Anderson & Co.

In about 1856 Dr. William Affleck Gray, an Edinburgh physician, bought the pottery and with his two sons, Alexander and William, used it to make exclusively stoneware. The name was altered to Midlothian Pottery. The Rathbones retained some interest in the firm.

In 1880 Gray & Co. purchased the Newbigging Pottery in nearby Musselburgh to produce once-fired white jam jars, taking out a patent on them in 1882. Dr. Gray died in 1896 but his sons carried on until William's death in 1919. The Works were now taken over by William Richardson who had worked there all of his life. He introduced a line in redware made from local clays.

Richardson died in 1925 and in 1926 the pottery was taken over by W.C. Bell, who had managed Caledonian Pottery in Rutherglen, but the Company quickly ran into the difficulties experienced by all the other stoneware potteries in the 1920s. The Company was re-organised, the Portobello works closed down and all production moved to Musselburgh but all to no avail since the Company was wound up in June 1928.

Under the Rathbones the pottery made pearlware and white earthenware, frequently transfer-printed but also painted. Both methods were used for the decoration of the usual range of domestic wares but a range of ornamental figures was made, enameled in very bright colours and immensely popular with east coast working people in both city and countryside. As well as this, it can be assumed that they made the usual range of factory slipwares: banded, mocha, machined, etc. As might be expected in view of the Rathbones' English connection, their transfer patterns are often derived from English originals.

The Grays seem to have concentrated on the most utilitarian of stonewares.

Pottery Descriptions: T.R. & Co. — printed or impressed
T. Rathbone P. — impressed
Gray — impressed
Gray & Co. — impressed

Reading: Quail, G. "Scottish Links with the Rathbones of Tunstall." in *SPHR* 14 (1992): 76-87.

26.1. Plate: The Font Rathbone period — copied from a Spode pattern — 9.50" diam. (£40/$70).

26.2. Storage jar, approx. 10" ht. (£40/$70), whisky flagon (£30/$50), jam jar (£5/$8).

26.3. Lidded butter dish, approx. 7.50" ht. (£40/$70).

26.4. Hot water bottle (£20/$35), storage jar (£30/$50), bottle (£15/$25), jam jar (£5/$8).

27 Newbigging Pottery, Musselburgh

The Pottery was founded by 1801 in Musselburgh, east of Edinburgh, by William Reid, who had previously leased the Pottery in West Pans and worked in Bo'ness. He died in 1835, having been joined in the Pottery by his two sons, Robert and George, who carried on the works for some time. The Pottery is said to have employed 70 or 80 men and to have made earthenware and perhaps stoneware. There followed a long period when ownership is not very clearly known, but throughout this time the pottery was operating. Then in 1893 it was taken over by W.A.Gray & Sons who made stoneware and already had works at Portobello nearby. The body made was now stoneware and the pottery continued making this until 1928 when Gray withdrew. The works may have run on for a little time after this, operated by a man named Reid, but this is uncertain.

An excavation carried out in 1980 and 1981 on the site of the Newbigging Pottery recovered many sherds of earthenware, decorated with transfer prints, sprigs, coloured slip banding, mocha, sponge-printing and lustre. Known marked pieces give little idea of the variety of wares made in Musselburgh which cover an enormous range and, until more complete pieces have been identified, the excavation reports are essential reading, particularly the discussion and illustration of the sherds in *SPHR* 18.

Pottery Descriptions: W. Reid
Wm. Reid — both painted
W. Reid — printed
Musselburgh Pottery — painted
Esk Pottery Co. — impressed.
Gray

Reading: Haggerty, George. "Newbigging Pottery" in *SPHR* 18 (1996): 15-38.

Haggerty and McIntyre. "Excavation report" in *Proceedings of the Society of Antiquaries of Scotland* 126 (1996): 943-962. These two are essential for an understanding of the site, the products and as a correction for older errors.

Quail, G. in *SPHR* 6 (1981): 85 and 10 (1986): 58-72 and McVeigh, P. "Scottish East Coast Potteries 1750-1840", pp. 94-103, both must be read in conjunction with the first two entries.

Pots at the Pans — catalogue — Newtongrange 1990

27.1. Hand-painted square plate — no mark (£60/$100).

27.2. Two moulded jugs marked Esk Pottery Co., Musselburgh, 7" ht.(£100/$170 each).

28

North British Pottery, Glasgow

This Pottery was founded about 1861 in Dobbie's Loan in central Glasgow by Robert Hedderwick Penman as the Osley Pottery, to make sanitary and general earthenware and water filters. His partners were Joseph Brown, a potter, and John W. Oslear, who is so far otherwise untraced. The site was quite close to the Glasgow Pottery, the City Glassworks (makers of Clutha glass) and the Cut of Junction Canal, which joined the Rivers Clyde and Forth across the narrowest part of Scotland. The Penman family were glass and ceramic retailers in the City.

In 1863 the firm stopped advertising sanitary wares, claiming only to be general earthenware manufacturers. In 1865 Joseph Brown and John W. Oslear both resigned from the partnership and Robert Penman carried on alone. In 1867, however, Penman had changed his address and the pottery appears in the Post Office Directory as D.Smith, jun. & Co., though still as the Osley Pottery. D. Smith, jun. is probably the son of a pawnbroker and himself an oil and candle merchant.

His tenure of the pottery cannot have been a success because by 1868 the pottery has been bought by James Miller & Co. James Miller was well-known on the pottery scene as the owner of Port Dundas Pottery which made stoneware very successfully. His partner in the new venture was one William Grant. They changed the name of the works to the North British Pottery which name was retained for the rest of its existence.

In 1874 the pottery was sold to Alexander Balfour who had been manager and then partner in Verreville Pottery, also in Glasgow. Miller continued to run Port Dundas Pottery and the Crown Pottery and William Grant remained as Balfour's partner until 1891. Balfour continued as owner until 1904 when the entire Pottery was purchased by the Caledonian Railway Co. for £18,500. It was destroyed in order to provide better access to their repair shop across the Canal. Balfour continued as an export merchant in earthenware, china and glass until 1914.

The only identified piece from the Penman period is a small two-handled tureen in white earthenware with a lilac transfer-printed border. From the Miller period there are fair numbers of white earthenware pieces decorated with transfer prints, sometimes with overglaze clobbering (28.1, 3, 4). His favoured pottery description was J.M. & Co., which is the same as that for one period of Bo'ness Pottery. Luckily in this case the J.M. & Co. is frequently accompanied by NORTH BRITISH POTTERY so that over the years any confusion has been cleared up (28.2).

From the Balfour period much the same sort of wares are known, though in much greater quantity. Pitchers seem to have been a speciality of the Works (28.6-8). Fleming states that Balfour produced bowls for the West African market decorated in hand-painting and with mottoes on them. The pottery was packed in empty palm-oil casks which were rolled over large tracts of land in Nigeria and neighbouring countries. When emptied, the casks were filled with palm oil and returned to Britain. Only one of these bowls has ever been identified in Scotland and none has been recorded as a return from Africa.

Balfour, and probably Miller, produced large quantities of sponge-printed and hand-painted wares but, since these were never marked, they have never been identified. Only transfer-printed earthenware has been identified from the North British Pottery; it remains for its spongeware to be named with any certainty (28.9).

Pottery Descriptions: all transfer-printed

R.H.P. & Co.
J.M. & Co.
North British Pottery
A.B. & Co.

Reading: Quail, G. "Osley & North British Pottery" in *Scottish Pottery Society's Pamphlet No.1* (1976)

Pattern List:

JM = recorded during Miller period. AB = recorded during Balfour period.

Acorn — JM & AB
Balmoral — floral — AB
Bertie's Hope — a boy dressed as a sailor — AB
Bramble — JM
Cherry Ripe — JM
Chinese — AB
Dahlia — dahlias — AB
Dawn — AB
Flora — JM
Fountain — AB
Hexagon — AB
Indian Flower — AB
Ivy — AB
My Pet — AB
Oporto — JM & AB
Portland — flower and vase — AB
Rustic — AB
Stork — AB
Swan — AB
Vintage — JM
Willow — AB
Windsor — same as Elgin Pottery pattern — AB

28.3 & 4. Punch bowl: Flora, 9.75" wide (£120/$200).

28.1. Ewer and basin with Flora pattern: ewer, 14.50" ht. (£100/$170 the set). Pitchers: Vintage, 7.50" ht. (£70/$120) and Bramble, 8" ht. (£70/$120).

28.2. Mark on Vintage.

28.5. Plate: Oporto, 9.50" (330/$50). Platter: Acorn, 16" lgth. (£40/$70).

28.7. Pitchers: Rustic, 7.50" ht. & Chinese, 8.25" ht. (£60/$100 each).

28.9. Bowl: sponge-printed, unmarked. Perhaps belonging to the North British Pottery and probably destined for the African market (£120/$200).

28.6. Pitchers: Indian Flower, 8.25" ht.; My Pet, 8.25" & 7.50" ht. (£70/$120 each).

28.8. Pitcher: Swan, 8" ht. (£70/$120).

29

Painting Ladies — the Glasgow Girls and Early Art Potteries

Towards the end of the nineteenth century, the Glasgow School of Art, under the able leadership of Fra Newbury, began to admit female students on an equal footing with male. The women of the first generation were all middle-class and mostly extremely talented. Many of them pursued subsequent careers in art, whether married or single, very successfully. They included painters, sculptors, potters, jewelers, workers in metal, embroiderers and many of them worked in several of these media. Some of them painted pottery but it must be understood that these painters did not make their own wares but functioned simply as independent decorators outside the industry. They bought blanks from many sources and had them glazed and fired also by commercial potteries. Some of them also ran classes to teach amateurs to decorate blanks and this had become a mania by the 1920s. Still, huge amounts of china and earthenware exist signed with initials or with some mark of the painter on the base. But for the professionals, The Glasgow Girls, the painted pottery was often an important source of income.

The most illustrious of these pottery painters as an artist (though not necessarily as a ceramic decorator) was Jessie Marion King. Born in 1875 in Bearsden, a middle-class dormitory suburb of Glasgow, she enrolled at Glasgow School of Art (G.S.A) in 1892. She was launched very quickly into an international career as painter and book illustrator and in 1906 was appointed Tutor in Ceramic Decoration at the G.S.A., a position she held for just one year. She lived at various times in Manchester and Paris but from 1945 the family headquarters was in Kirkcudbright in southern Scotland. From then onwards she constantly decorated both china and earthenware. Her blanks were obtained from many sources. It has been claimed that most came from Methven's of Kirkcaldy but this seems unlikely since many of her pieces are made of china, which was never made in that Pottery. Some of the pieces undoubtedly come from there and could have been glazed and fired there. Her usual mark is in three parts: her initials JMK, a green gate (her house in Kirkcudbright was called Greengates) and a rabbit (there was a life sized stone rabbit in her garden).

Her decoration is usually very delicate with her brilliant observation of plants and animals but it can be occasionally 'bitty'. Latterly she sometimes indulged in a very unattractive dark blue which can totally unbalance her compositions. Her repertoire includes flowers, animals and children, fairies and nursery rhymes, but extends to many other subjects in the pieces she painted to order or for friends.

Probably the most illustrious of the women as a pottery painter was Elizabeth Mary Watt. Born in Dundee in 1885, she came at the age of nineteen or twenty to Glasgow where, apart from a year spent between Sheffield and London, she passed the rest of her life until her death in 1954. She never married but supported herself entirely by her painting and ceramic decoration.

Her work falls into several categories. She was known for her portraits of children but her subject matter in painting was very varied. Her blanks came from potteries all over Europe. On earthenware her designs are bold and assured, the shapes are often outlined in blue or black. Subjects range widely from elves and toadstools to totally abstract designs. On china her painting is more delicate, frequently taking the form of flowers in pink and blue against a pale yellow background. She signed her work with her initials EMW, often intertwined.

Ann Macbeth painted earthenware and porcelain from a vast variety of sources. Her speciality was a tangerine lustre. Many of her designs carried heavy outlines and her repertoire is more limited than that of Elizabeth Mary Watt. Embroidery had been her first craft and she, in fact, taught that subject at G.S.A. From 1913 to 1922 ceramic decoration was added to embroidery as teaching subject. From then until 1948 she lived in the Lake District in north west England though she continued to exhibit ceramics and embroidery with the Society of Lady Artists in Glasgow.

The list of Glasgow Girls could be added to almost indefinitely. Mary Fairgrieve, The Walton sisters, Dorothy Carleton Smyth, De Courcy Lewthwaite Dewar, Annie French and Helen Paxton Brown all have a reputation for producing work in the Art Nouveau style in one medium or another and all are known to have decorated pottery. With the Charles Rennie Mackintosh group and Talwyn Morris, they must take much of the credit for creating the Glasgow Style.

One of the graduates from GSA worked mainly in Edinburgh. Elizabeth Amour came from a Border family and attended GSA from 1908 till 1912. By the next year she had married and settled in Edinburgh where she founded the Bough Pottery along with four other members of her family. The Bough bought blanks from a number of sources and each member of the family signed each piece with their initials in addition to the word BOUGH. The enterprise was successful and continued fully operative until 1942, though Christine Amour continued to paint ceramics until 1960 without the word BOUGH in the mark. Bough's work was always underglaze.

A unique development of the painted pottery movement was the Mak'Merry Studio founded near Macmerry in East Lothian about 1919. The founder was Catherine Blair, a farmer's wife, a suffragette and a founder of the Scottish Women's Rural Institute. She and a few helpers took lessons in painting pottery and founded their business from scratch. Blanks were bought from Glasgow, Bo'ness, Kirkcaldy and England. Many were fired at Bo'ness. Later the Studio moved to North Berwick in the same county, where it functioned until the late 1930s.

From some time in the early 1920s until 1940, three graduates from GSA—Mary Ramsay, Jessie Wilson and Maggie McDonald—decorated china and earthenware bought as blanks in the Studio in Strathyre in Perthshire. The pots came from many sources but were fired at Bo'ness. Most of the decoration was floral. Pieces were often signed with painted initials and the word STRATHYRE. A shortage of blanks put an end to production in 1940.

The men who took up 'art ceramics' in this period tended to become full potters and often to use coloured glazes for decoration rather than hand-painted designs.

Hugh 'Ugolino' Allan was born in 1862 in Glasgow, son of a master builder and brickmaker. He graduated from GSA in 1885 with a Teacher's Certificate and pursued a career as a painter until 1902. In that year Robert McLaurin of the Scottish Guild of Handicraft Ltd. persuaded him to attempt pottery making. Allan built a studio in the village of Milngavie to the north of Glasgow; his kiln was built by Robert McLaurin. Allan had no training in pottery and was completely self-taught in all techniques. He was subject to asthma which prevented him from working in the studio during the winter months, so the amount of work he produced in his six years' operation is not large.

Mostly he made vases, bowls and jardinieres. His use of translucent and crystalline glazes is remarkable and frequently very beautiful. The Pottery was given up in 1908 and Allan died in the following year.

Henry Taylor Wyse was born in Glasgow but at a very young age moved with his family to Dundee. He took a Teacher's Certificate from the Art School there but subsequently moved to the Glasgow area so as to study at GSA. This was followed by a short study period in Paris and teaching in various schools in the East of Scotland, latterly in Edinburgh.

A successful career as a painter lead to furniture design and by the turn of the century he was a member of the Guild of Handicraft Ltd. He wrote and published several books on craftwork. About 1918 he founded a small pottery where the throwing of wares was done by an assistant and the glazing was largely experimental. The Pottery was known as the Holyrood.

Success was followed by the buying in of blanks for decoration by glazing but biscuit wares were also sold to the public and fired for them. The mark on their own wares was an impressed HOLYROOD with a cross within a circle, the foot of the cross jutting out of the circle. Throughout this period, Wyse continued teaching and from 1922 worked at the training of teachers. The Pottery was sold off but continued until 1931.

William Miles Johnston was born in Edinburgh in 1893, trained at the Edinburgh College of Art then in the U.S.A. and returned to Scotland to teach in Edinburgh schools. He had studied for a time with Jessie M. King in Kirkcudbright and in 1940 moved there to live.

Between 1925 and 1940 he painted blanks bought mostly from Bo'ness. His main theme was animals of all kinds, often with borders of radiating lines. His mark was a monogram in a circle and the word ZOO painted on the base. After 1940 the wartime shortage of blanks meant that he had to give up decorating Zoo Ware, though he decorated some glass.

Reading: Cruickshank, G. "The Zoo Pottery" in *Scottish Pottery Society Archive News* 4 (1979): 32-38.

Dickson, Kay. "The Studio, Strathyre" in *SPHR* 13 (1989): 1-12.

Hill, Robin. "Mak'Merry Blanks and Decorators" in *Scottish Home & Country* for December 1987

King horn, Jonathan. "Glasgow Style Ceramics" in *SPHR* 9(1985): 17-31.

______. "Glasgow Style Postscript" in *SPHR* 10 (1986): 32.

______. "Hugh Ugolino Allan" in *Milngavie & Bearsden Herald* for October 10 1986
Kinghorn & Quail. "The Holyrood Pottery" in *SPHR* 10 (1985): 34-39.
Moffat Nan. "Muirhead Round the Studios" — reprint *Milngavie* 1982
Scott-Sutherland, C. *Elizabeth Mary Watt* — Newmill 1995
White, C. *The Enchanted World of Jessie M. King* — Edinburgh 1989
Jessie M. *King and E.A. Taylor* —sale catalogue— Sotheby's 1977
Glasgow Society of Lady Artists 1882 —catalogue— Glasgow 1982
The Glasgow Style (1890-1920) —catalogue— Glasgow 1984

29.1. JMK: Nursery rhyme plate, approx. 7" diam. (£600/$1000)

29.2. JMK: John Paul Jones and ship plate (a pair), 6.50" diam. (£1000/ $1700 the pair). Lidded bowl (£500/$835).

29.4. JMK: Ash tray - elf with mushrooms, approx. 3.50" diam. (£500/ 835). Wall vase with swallows and flowers (£600/$1000). Ash tray with foxgloves, approx. 3.50" diam. (£600/$1000).

29.3. JMK: Mowgli vase (£3000/$5100) and water lily vase (£1000/$1700).

29.5. JMK: Foxglove mark.

29.6. JMK: Mermaid vase (£3000/$5100). Floral vase (£2500/$3175). Floral pitcher, approx. 4.75" ht. (£600/$1000).

29.7. JMK: Handled mugs, approx. 4.50" ht. (£500/$835 each). Small plate (£500/$835).

29.8. JMK: Handled jugs, approx. 4.50" ht. (£500/$835 each). Soup plate with underdish (£600/$1000).

29.9. JMK: Small lidded box (£450/$750). Lidded box with bee (£550/$920). Sugar shaker (£500/$835).

29.10. JMK: Small mug (£500/$835). Large mug with inscription WHEN ADAM DELVED AND EVE SPAN WHO WAS THEN THE GENTLEMAN? (£700/1200). Plate with figure (£600/$1000).

29.11. JMK: Wares with a large amount of dark blue. Pitcher, approx. 5" ht. (£500/$835). Plate (£450/$750). Two-handled dish (£450/$750).

29.12. JMK: Stone rabbit from Jessie Marion King's garden in Kirkudbright, approx. 5" ht..

29.13. EMW: Ash tray, elf and mushrooms, approx. 3" diam. (£90/$150).

29.15. EMW: China cup and saucer (£80/$135), lidded bowl (£90/$150), and small plate (£70/$120).

29.14. EMW: Pixie quaich (£120/$200) and coffee cup and saucer (£80/$135).

29.16. EMW: China sandwich plate (£80/$135) and wooden finger plate from door (£150/250).

29.17. Mark from photo 29.16.

29.18. AMB: Armistice Day mug, approx. 3.75" ht. (£150/$250), Patterdale lidded dish (£ 100/$170), and small lustred dish, 2.75" lgth. (£50/$85).

29.20. Mark.

29.19. AMB: Cup & saucer (£60/$100) and vase with lustre (£140/$235).

29.21. Allander Pottery: large pot, 9.50" ht. (£200/$340).

29.22. Allander Pottery: large pot, 9.50" ht. (£150/$250).

29.23. Allander Pottery: plate (£170/$285).

29.24. Allander Pottery: mark.

29.25. Bough: pitcher, 6.25" ht. (£100/$170).

29.26. Bough: coffee set (£90/$150).

29.27. Makmerry: small dish (£35/$60) and creamer, approx. 5" ht. (£50/$85).

29.28. Zoo Pottery: creamer (£130/$220).

29.29. A selection of pieces by unknown painters. Soup plate, 6.25" ht. mono-grammed J. H. M. (£20/$35); vase, 8" ht. monogrammed M. R. C. (£30/$50); bowl, 3.50" diam., L.M.H. (£25/$40); jam pot, 4" ht. LESWALT painted (£35/$60).

30

Port Dundas Pottery, Glasgow

So far as current research has determined, the Port Dundas Pottery Co. as a continuously functioning firm was founded in 1828, though earlier the name had been used at other sites. Port Dundas was the area round a basin formed where a branch of the Forth & Clyde Canal joined the Monkland Canal. This was then just to the north of Glasgow but is now almost part of the City centre. The Monkland Canal brought coal from the north Lanarkshire coalfield and the other Canal joined the area to both coasts of Scotland via the rivers Clyde and Forth, giving easy access to export markets. Port Dundas consequently became a very highly industrialised suburb with metal-working, distilling, acid-making and pottery firms among many others.

The builder and owner of the pottery was William Johnstone, who was in partnership with John Forsyth and John McColl, the last of whom was a potter. The products were salt-glazed stonewares, mainly bottles for local manufacturers.

In 1835 Johnstone sold the pottery to another group of businessmen. Robert Cochran and James Couper were already partners in a glass and china retail outlet and John McColl stayed on as pottery manager. In 1837 John McColl left but the other two carried on for two more years before, in 1839, selling Port Dundas Pottery and buying the St. Rollox Glass Works.

The Pottery was bought by George Duncan who, however, died in 1841 and there followed a period of obscurity in which the names of his widow Helen and a potter called Alexander Paul figure prominently. James Miller was for some time the manager and, in 1856, in partnership with John Moody, he bought the Works.

Miller was a man of immense energy. He changed from salt-glazing to using the new Bristol glaze which did much less damage to kilns and he streamlined the production of draining pipes, which had become a speciality of the Firm. In the face of opposition from the potters, he mechanised the Works, abolishing the need for wheel turners for the pottery wheels. Under Miller, the range of products was greatly enlarged. Bottles (of course), whisky and acid jars as well as casks, butter pots, jam jars and a vast array of domestic wares were made. Port Dundas water filters became popular and so successful that a special part of the Works was built to make them. They had a world-wide distribution, as witness a gold medal award in Chile in 1875.

In the 1860s Port Dundas was one of the firms using Donaldson Brothers' Shipping Line to export to South America and the Pacific Rim. From the 1870s on, there was an enormous trade by the pottery in beer bottles for South American brewers, bearing the name of the brewery printed or impressed or on a light blue applied pad. In 1867 Miller expanded his concern by buying the North British Pottery to make whiteware and carried it on successfully with a partner until 1874, when it was sold.

In 1875 Miller, in partnership with John Young, leased part of the old Caledonian Pottery and, as Crown Pottery, made a range of splash-glazed plates and caneware baking dishes until the premises burnt down in 1879. On the owners refusal to repair the buildings this enterprise closed down.

However, by the 1880s Young was working in the main Pottery on the re-introduction of salt-glazing on a range of whisky jugs in art forms. These displayed a great range of shapes; some were long-necked and decorated with sgraffito papyrus leaves with blue coloring rubbed in, some were moulded as cabbages or with overall knobbles. One jug is known moulded with Egyptian motifs and brightly enameled.

Also in the early 1880s, an extension to the Works was built across the way. This was known as Milton Pottery. Maps of the period show the Port Dundas Pottery as having nine kilns and Milton, an additional four. In 1905 Miller's son, James W., was taken into partnership and Milton Pottery began to make electrical insulators in the usual porcelain. In the same year, Miller died but the family carried the Pottery on as a limited liability company.

By 1929 the pottery was owned by Borax Consolidated Ltd., but it closed down in 1930 as most uses for stoneware were now dying, replaced by other materials such as glass and rubber. Some of the plant and goodwill were sold to Possil Pottery, but by 1932 the affairs of the Company had been finally and completely wound up.

Pottery Descriptions: Port Dundas Pottery Co.

Reading: Kelly, H.E. "Possil Pottery etc." in *SPHR* 17 (1995): 36-60.

______. "Caledonian Railway Map" in *SPHR* 16 (1994): 35-37.

______. "The Life of Robert Cochran of Britannia and Verreville Potteries" in *Scottish Industrial History* 18 (1996): 8-28.

Leishman, D.A. "The Port Dundas Pottery Company" in *SPHR* 19 (1997): 19-28.

Quail, G. "Pottery at Port Dundas" in *Pottery and Craft Gazette* (1982)

30.1. Butter dishes, approx. 6.50" ht. (£40-45/$70-75); whisky flagon (£30/$50) with customers' names and addresses

30.2. Acid jar, 18" ht. (£50/$85), whisky flagon, 10" ht.(£30/$50), and large whisky barrel, 21" ht. (£90/$150).

30.3. Hunting pitcher (£40/$70), hot water bottle (£30/$50) and whisky bottle with flattened sides (£45/$75).

30.4. Two jars, 12", one with salt glaze (£50/$85), one with "Bristol" or borax glaze(£35/$60), creamer of brown catering ware (£10/$17).

30.5. Two whisky flagons, approx. 7" ht. (£70/$120 each) and salt glazed pitcher, approx. 6" ht. (£50/$85).

30.6. Water filter with dome lid missing, 16" ht. (£120/$200).

30.7. Salt glazed art wares: two whisky flagons, 6.75" and 8.50" ht. (£400/$680 each), one with incised initials J. D. Y., and pitcher with side handle (£80/$135).

30.8. Impressed mark.

30.9. Plate, moulded and splash glazed made by Miller and Young at the Crown Pottery, 9.75" diam. (£40/$70).

31

Possil or Saracen Pottery, Glasgow

No Scottish pottery has had a more varied history than this — its name was changed as well as its products. Starting life in a humble way as a maker of colored wares, it was elevated to making some of the finest porcelain ever made in Britain and then sank to being a manufacturer of beer bottles.

The four-kiln pottery was founded in 1875 as Bayley, Murray and Brammer. The partners formed a combination of potters and businessmen and the pottery was known at this time as the Saracen Pottery. Joseph Brammer was an earthenware painter and Methodist local preacher according to the 1871 Census. The wares made at first had coloured bodies or glazes, principally teapots and pitchers with other household goods in Rockingham, cane, black basalte, jet and mazarin blue, though at some time coarse white ware was made, though never advertised.

Over the twenty-one years of its first period there were many changes of partnership, even legal disputes, goods were exhibited at the 1888 Glasgow Exhibition and were even exported, a switch was made to stoneware manufacture, and the name was changed to Possil Pottery. Possil was the district of Glasgow in which the company stood and this name was to stay with the pottery for the rest of its life. It closed in 1896.

Meanwhile, in the centre of the City, a very successful firm of china wholesalers and retailers had decided to set up their own works and had rented, in 1894, part of a stoneware pottery. They were called MacDougall & Sons, but at this date the sole partners were two brothers called MacDougall. Their aim was to make porcelain of the finest quality and in this they succeeded. The products have similarities to Limoges, Worcester and Belleek's wares, but how they obtained or trained their workers is still not fully known. In 1896 they purchased the empty Possil Pottery, altered it and moved in.

Dessert wares, tea sets and ornamental wares in hand-painted porcelain were their principal products. The body was incredibly fine, sometimes approximating to egg-shell china; the painting was of very high quality. Only the design is over-elaborate in a late Victorian-Edwardian manner, but this fault is not evident in the figurines or in the tea or dessert sets, which are exquisite. Woven baskets were made but are usually unmarked and often attributed to Belleek, who also made them with a very similar glaze. They named their ware 'Nautilus Porcelain' and, though shell ornaments were made in great numbers, nautilus shells are never found. A subsidiary line was crested wares, of which there is an enormous variety. These, too, were marked 'Nautilus Porcelain'.

Earthenware was also made: hand-painted, transfer printed and sponge printed. This is always marked 'Possil Pottery' or 'Possil Pottery Co.' with the cursive M which is found on many of their wares. One earthenware product was bedroom sets which were painted in the same manner as the porcelain.

The death of one brother in 1910 may have precipitated the closure of the pottery, which took place in 1911.

The buildings were to stand empty until 1916, when they were bought by Tennents — a firm of brewers in Glasgow — in order to help with the drastic wartime scarcity of stoneware beer bottles for the Cuban market. The company formed to run the pottery was known as 'Glasgow Trading and Transport Ltd.' — a subsidiary of Tennents with the same board of directors.

Over the years economic difficulties were encountered and to cope with this the range of wares was greatly extended to include foot warmers (i.e. hot water bottles), acid and varnish bottles, whisky jars, jam pots, cream jars and electrical insulators. In fact, in 1938 they supplied the electrical insulators for the transatlantic liner the 'Queen Elizabeth'.

In 1936 a range of art wares in unglazed white stoneware was launched. This was known as Possil Ware and its principal retail outlet was an arts and crafts shop in London. It is now extremely rare. A range of brown catering ware was also made but the complexities involved with running the pottery during the Second World War, with the shortage of raw materials and man power, were too much for the board and, in 1942, the site was sold to an iron works.

A curious postscript to the history of Nautilus Porcelain is provided by the Coral Porcelain Co. of Prestonpans. This company was founded by John Boyle and Daniel Harrigan on the closure of the Possil Pottery by the MacDougall Brothers. John Boyle had worked at Beleek and Possil; Harrigan was a Glasgow glass and china importer who provided the capital. Boyle seems to have brought copper plates and moulds from Possil and, for a short time, made imitations of Nautilus, their souvenirs, and probably their earthenware. The partnership was brought to an end by a court action in 1915.

Pottery Descriptions: B.M. & B. impressed or printed
Saracen Pottery printed
Nautilus Porcelain printed
Possil Pottery Co. printed
Possil Pottery painted
Possil Ware stamped

Reading: Kelly, H.E. "Possil Pottery, Tennent and Glasgow Trading & Transport Ltd." in *SPHR* 17 (1995): 36-60.

Leishman, D.A. & Turnbull, J. "Nautilus Porcelain Figures" in *SPHR* 17 (1995): 30-35.

Quail, G. *Nautilus Porcelain* - Glasgow 1983 - care must be taken in reading section 3, which is full of inaccuracies.

31.1. Porcelain: figure of a water carrier, 21" ht. (£1500/$2500).

31.2. Detail of the porcelain displayed in image 31.1.

31.3. Colored figure of a water carrier, 13" ht. (£1000+/$1700+).

31.4. Female figure pairing with 31.3, 13" ht. (£1000+/$1700+).

31.5. Nude female figure, 14.75″ ht. (£1000+/$1700+).

31.6. Nymph and shell, 14″ wide 11″ ht. (£1100+/£1800+).

31.7. Shell with boy, girl and rabbit, 12.75″ ht. (£800/$1340).

31.8. Boy beside rustic basin, 1[illegible].50″ ht. (£500-800/$835-1340).

31.9. Pair of shells with children, 8.25″ lgth. (£700/$1170).

31.10. Tall, slender vases, 12″ ht. (£400/$670).

31.11. Vase with dragon handles, 12" ht. (£1000/$1670).

31.12. Loving cup with three anthropomorphic handles, 6" ht., 6" diam. (£1000/$1670).

31.14. Large pot 15" diam., 11" ht. (£800-1200/$1340-2100).

31.13. Jardiniere with dragon handles, 19" lgth. (£1000/$1670).

31.15. Pair of vases, 7.50 ht. (£1200/$2100 pair).

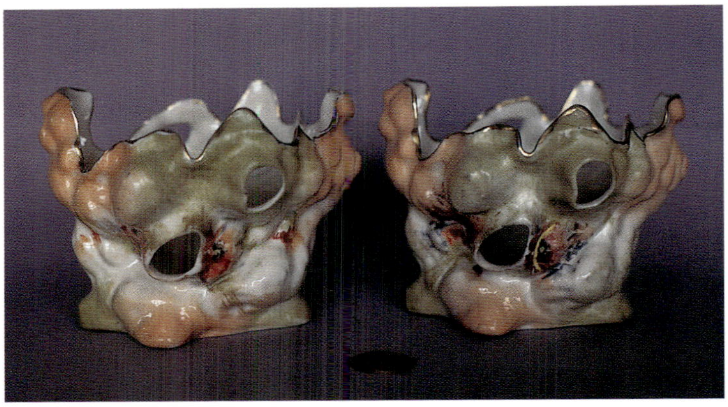

31.16. Rustic bowls, 5.75" diam. (£900/$1500 pair).

31.17. Vases with marine scenes, 8" ht. (£1000/$1670 pair).

31.18. Vases with painted narcissi, 15.75" ht. (£1500/$2500).

31.19. Twisted vase with child, 12" ht. (£1500/$2500).

31.20. Vases with painted roses, 12.75" ht. (£900/$1500).

31.21. Tea set with gilding: cup, 3.50" diam.; plate, 7" diam. (£360/$610)

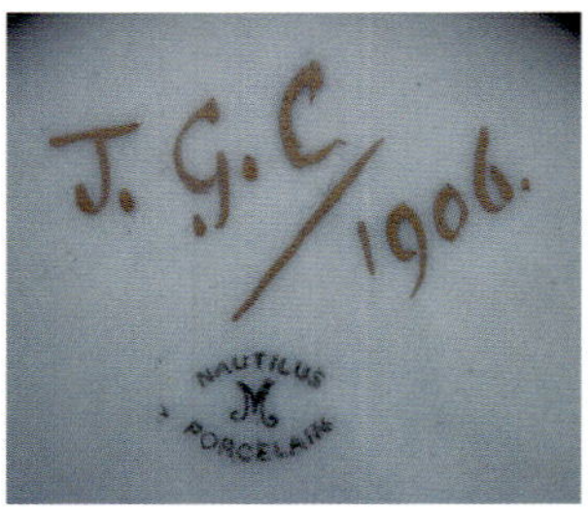

31.22. Mark on tea set shown in 31.21.

31.23. Two trios: cups, 3" & 3.50" diam. (£60/$100 each)

31.24. Part of harlequin tea set: bread plate, 8.75" diam.; tea plate, 6.75" diam. (£300/$500 for six places)

31.25. Porcelain souvenirs: tallest, 4.50" ht. (£25-30/$40-50)

31.26. Two pieces of Coral Porcelain. Cup: 3" diam. (£10/$17). Plate: approx. 7" diam. (£15/$25)

31.27. Earthenware: small bowl, approx. 3" diam. (£10/$17) and plate, 9.75" diam. (£35/$60)

31.28. Pitcher, approx. 9" ht. (£25/$40) and painted and sponge-printed plate, 10.50" diam. (£50/$85).

31.29. Possil Ware vase, 9.75" ht. (£80/$135) and bleach bottle, 15.25" ht. (£40/$70).

31.30. Pneumatic trough, 9.50" diam. (£30/$50), whisky flagon (£60/$100), and side-handled pitcher (£40/$70).

31.31. Small whisky bottle, 4.75" ht. (£20/$35), and two water pitchers for a bar, souvenirs of the Glasgow Empire Exhibition of 1937-8, 3" ht. (£25/$40 each). The transfer on the whisky bottle has been damaged by water, showing that it was never fired.

32

The Auld Kirk Pottery, Prestonpans

There were two potteries in Prestonpans in the eighteenth century: the Auld Kirk and the much smaller Bankfoot. No wares have ever been positively identified from the Bankfoot.

The Auld Kirk Pottery was founded in 1750 by William Cadell, a very wealthy local businessman. It was built to make creamware, often with a tortoise-shell glaze, for export. The capital was £200, of which William Cadell contributed half for himself and another quarter for his nephew and namesake. The remaining quarter came from Samuel Garbet. Dr. John Roebuck, partner of William Cadell in several enterprises, could take no share in the partnership since he was still an undischarged bankrupt, but nevertheless played a part in running the business.

William Cadell had many lines of trade stretching to the Baltic coasts, to Leghorn in Italy, and even across the Atlantic to the West Indies. The creamware became another item in his trading repertoire, not perhaps of the greatest importance in the huge bulk of his business.

In 1774 William's nephew left to form the Bankfoot Pottery on his own and it is likely that William senior's two sons, William junior and John, joined the business at this time. Meanwhile, William senior and John Roebuck had moved to West Lothian and formed the Carron Iron Works, which became by far Cadell's most important business. William junior followed them, leaving John in charge of the Pottery. John also had a retail outlet in Edinburgh and from his advertisements we learn that the Auld Kirk was making "White, Cream, Black and Tortoise-shell ware."

Although large amounts of pottery were made and exported, there is evidence that it was not always of the highest quality. In fact, a Staffordshire potter who visited the works in 1786 poured scorn on both the organisation and the workmanship at the Auld Kirk.

In 1796 the pottery was sold, perhaps as a result of a drop in demand (or rather an inability to deliver) due to the war with France, which completely closed off the markets in Europe to British firms.

There were three partners in the new concern: John Fowler, a local brewer, distiller and farmer, David Thomson, a potter, and William Anderson, who had been clerk at the pottery for some time. Anderson withdrew a few years later. Creamware continued to be made, both transfer-printed and painted. The usual coloured slipwares were made: mocha, slip-banded, and machined. Goods are known to have been sent all over Scotland, but none has been certainly identified. Gradually the range of wares was extended to include jet and marbled wares and black basalte; lustre was added to the decorative techniques. A large range of brown-glazed goods was manufactured and it is possible that soft-paste porcelain was made.

After a very complex series of judicial processes, David Thomson was declared bankrupt and died shortly thereafter. In 1817 or 1819, the firm became Hamilton Watson & Co. Hamilton Watson had been working at the pottery for some years but it is thought that John Fowler had still some interest in the business. Watson presided over the decline and final demise of the pottery. He was declared bankrupt in 1838 and the pottery finally closed shortly thereafter.

There is a vast amount of detailed information still extant on the history and workings of the Auld Kirk Pottery. This contrasts very strongly with the very few pieces which can be attributed to the pottery with any degree of certainty at any period of its near-century of existence.

Pottery Descriptions: Presstounpan 1754 — incised
Watson — printed
Watson & Co. — printed

Reading: Quail, G. "The Old Kirk Pottery, Prestonpans" in *SPHR* 10 (1986): 58-72.
Pots at the Pans — catalogue — Newtongrange 1990

32.1. Transfer-printed plate, 6.25" diam. (£50/$85).

32.2. Mark on the transfer-printed plate in 32.1.

33

Rosslyn Pottery, Kirkcaldy

This was built in 1879 by Morrison & Crawford in Oswald Rd., Kirkcaldy. Adam Morrison had been the traveler for the Links Pottery and Crawford had been their kilnman, so between them they were well qualified to run their own business. Unfortunately Crawford died very shortly after the foundation but Morrison continued on his own as Morrison & Crawford.

In 1883 a more modern pottery was required and was built close by. In 1919 A. Hunter, Morrison's nephew, took over as proprietor after having worked with his uncle for some time. In 1926 he leased the pottery out for five years and in 1932 closed it. The contents were auctioned off on 30 November of the same year.

Originally the pottery made Rockingham-glazed teapots, mostly thrown by hand, though some were cast in moulds. Majolica wares were also made in abundance and are, in fact, the best known product of the Rosslyn Pottery. Many storage barrels are found with raised legends: RICE, MEAL, CEREAL, FLOUR, etc. Bread bins were made as well as "pirley" banks in the shapes of animals, buildings, etc. Cane ware dishes were made for kitchen use.

The majolica was glazed in brown, blue and green over a cane-coloured body. The colour was applied using twigs of broom or whin, which gives a more spotted effect than the similar splash-glazed wares made by Seaton Pottery in Aberdeen.

In 1924 a decline in trade led to the introduction of whiteware using imported clays from Cornwall. This ware was painted by Karel Nekola of Wemyss Ware fame. He also at this time decorated a new line in jet wares.

Pottery Descriptions: Morrison & Crawford

Reading: Insh, J. Rodger. *The Kirkcaldy Potteries* — Kirkcaldy 1974, reprinted 1982.
McNeill, Carol. *Kirkcaldy Potteries* — Kirkcaldy: Fife Publicity, 1998

33.1. Painted jardiniere, approx. 8" ht. (£55/$90).

33.2. Storage barrel with splashed glazes. In contrast with the Seaton splashed glaze barrels the lettering is raised above the general level of the piece, 9.50" ht. (£60/$100)

34

Scottish Jugs

What are called jugs in Great Britain are known as pitchers in the U.S.A. Nevertheless I shall refer to them in this chapter as jugs since I am talking of Scotland and the place of jugs in the life of working class and lower middle class Scots was very special. Jugs functioned as the housewife's art gallery and sometimes very large collections were put together. It was not too unusual to have over a hundred in one kitchen.

Jugs were given as Christmas presents (indeed there were special Christmas jugs for that purpose). More unusually, there are also jugs for New Year, birthdays and Valentine's Day. Jugs, and sets of jugs, were given as wedding presents and often to favoured farm servants at the end of their year's 'hiring'.

The 'Sets' in Scotland most often consisted of two matching jugs but in the late nineteenth century, when German and English jugs were replacing Scots-made, 'sets' meant three jugs matching in pattern and shape but graduated in size. Frequently special inscriptions were written on to the jug. This could be done in the pottery of origin but independent firers and decorators existed in some numbers. They would glaze, inscribe, and fire, or refire, your jug for you. These independent firers and decorators certainly existed until the 1950s and may yet exist today.

The high point for the Scots jug is the second half of the nineteenth century. Before this, jugs were, of course, made and used but they tended to conform to English habits and show real or fantastic and lacustrine landscapes. This is not surprising, since there must still have been many English potters employed in the Scottish potteries. After 1860, the Scots jug really comes into its own and the reason for its popularity becomes obvious. The subject matter of the transfers with which it was most often decorated expands enormously. Politicians, opera singers, flowers (domestic and exotic), animals (ditto.), royal weddings and coronations, oriental scenes, rat-catching, children playing, bull-fighting, international exhibitions, fashion plates, famous paintings, Highland landscapes, pottery, military scenes, allegorical figures and figures from literature are among the subjects dealt with.

Most of the patterns are transfer prints and many of them are clobbered with enamels above the glaze; many also have an amber lustre, often called an iron lustre. In Scotland this always seems to have a more tangerine shade than the yellower shade it has on English pots.

Certain potteries seem to have specialised in jugs which, judging by survivals, made up a fair percentage of their output. Of course, since these jugs were so highly thought of, it is possible that to a certain extent we are dealing with preferential survival; however, even so, Clyde Pottery, Victoria Pottery and Britannia seem to have produced more jugs than the others, as will be seen in the illustrations to this volume.

Christmas pottery may well have originated with Bells' dinner ware pattern Holly Wreath of the 1870s. If so, it is strange that Bells' never followed up this profitable line. The first Christmas jugs seem to have been produced by Clyde Pottery and Bo'ness Pottery, but the latter again did not pursue this line of ware which other potteries found so profitable. Clyde Pottery and Britannia are those with the most surviving Christmas jugs but Victoria, Links and Bridgeness all produced some. Now, the production of Christmas wares has become an international phenomenon.

The popularity of the jug in Scotland seems to have died simultaneously with the demise of the Scottish potteries, which succumbed to world depression, foreign competition, railway expansion and world wars over a period of fifty years or more. Now the collections have been dispersed and we can only be glad that so many specimens still exist to illustrate the creativity shown by Scots in an industry which Scots are once again beginning to appreciate.

35

Seaton Pottery, Aberdeen

Very few Scottish potteries, as opposed to brick and tileworks, were ever founded outside Scotland's central belt and, of those that were, almost all produced redware, stoneware or fireclay. Seaton Pottery is no exception, being a typical country redware pottery, although it existed on the edge of a bustling, prosperous city.

It was founded in 1868 by Thomas Gavin and James Ritchie. Gavin was a potter who had come from Glasgow about eighteen years before and functioned as a wine and spirit merchant throughout the rest of his life. Less is known about Ritchie, who came from Prestonpans. The Pottery had one kiln and eight workmen. Ritchie quickly faded from the scene and was replaced by Gavin's two sons, Hugh and John. The Pottery functioned until Thomas Gavin's death in 1899 but closed in 1903.

In 1904, however, it was re-opened by two potters from Denby in Derbyshire, Clark and Smith. They lasted only until 1905. Arthur Mills had come from Denby to work for Clark and Smith and, on their failure, he took over the pottery. He was joined in 1915 by his son Ivor who ran the pottery after 1927. Gradually the output was restricted in type until the pottery produced only flower pots and with the advent of plastic flower pots the pottery lost its trade and closed in 1964.

In its first period, and indeed almost throughout its life, the pottery produced all the usual redwares associated with such potteries and, like the others, did not mark them so that they are now virtually unidentifiable. However, over the years the Gavins produced some easily recognisable products, mostly of a rather more expensive nature. During the 1880s their speciality was agate ware in shades of brown and white with a honey coloured glaze. Storage barrels, butter dishes, chicken-shaped penny banks and pilgrim flasks were amongst the commonest shapes. These are very often distinguished by a shield-shaped sprig with inlaid white lettering giving a name and date. They also made large bowls with sgrafitto patterns including names and dates. In the 1890s these gave way to wares with a splashed glaze in brown, green and blue. The inlaid, brown lettering was now set against a white background.

Clark and Smith's wares were in the 'art' shapes of the period, often with variegated glazes. Vases are the commonest shapes but more utilitarian goods were made. At the outset of the third period, some large pieces were made for show but over the years the products were mostly flower pots and other utilitarian wares.

Pottery Descriptions: none from the first period
Clark and Smith impressed
Mills impressed

Reading: Cruickshank, G. "The Seaton Pottery" in *Aberdeen Ceramics* — Aberdeen, A.G. Museum 1981: 26-36.

"Seaton Art Pottery" in *Pottery Gazette and Glass Trade Review* for November 2 1908

35.1. Agate ware: pilgrim flask, 12.50" ht. (£160/$270); money bank, 4.25" lgth. (£50/$85); butter dish [lacking lid], 8.50" diam. (£90/$150); and storage barrel, 10.75" ht. (£130/$220).

35.2. Splash-glazed storage barrel, 9" ht. (£90/$150) and large bowl with sgraffito decoration, 16.50" diam. (£450/$750).

36

Sinclairtown Pottery, Kirkcaldy

The Sinclairtown Pottery was founded in Rosslyn St., Kirkcaldy, in 1869 by George McLauchlan. It employed 30 men and boys but went bankrupt in 1874 and was sold to David Kirk and his three sons, David, Andrew and Robert. In 1884 Robert was sole partner but on emigrating to Philadelphia he made the pottery over to his nephew James Buist, a Glasgow draper. James took his father Lawrence and brothers into the business, which traded as L. Buist & Sons.

About 1899 the Rosslyn Street site, which probably had only two kilns, was sold and a new Pottery erected in Oswald Road, which worked until about 1930 and then closed down for good.

Sinclairtown Pottery's staple product was undoubtedly Rockingham-glazed teapots. At the height of its production, the pottery was making 700 dozen a day. This is all the more remarkable when it is considered that much larger potteries like Caledonian were turning out similar, if not greater, numbers and Sinclairtown had to compete. Baking dishes, mugs and bowls were also made and there is a slight possibility that white sponge-printed wares were made.

Pottery Descriptions: Buist & Sons, fireproof, Kirkcaldy — impressed (only one marked piece known).

Reading: James, Heather, Turnbull, Gordon and Meechan, Dallas. *The Excavations at Sinclairtown Pottery, Kirkcaldy* — Kirkcaldy: Fife Regional Council, n.d. but c.1992

McNeill, Carol. *Kirkcaldy Potteries* — Kirkcaldy: Fife Publicity, 1998

36.1. Teapot with Rockingham glaze, 10.50" lgth. (£40/$70).

37

Spongeware

Sponge-printing seems to have been first used to decorate pottery in modern times somewhere in Scotland about 1835. The hard and uncommercial 'root' of a sponge was cut into a shape and usually glued to a handle. Enamel colour was laid in a saucer, a sherd, or a piece of leather, and the biscuit ware, on a wheel, was decorated much as a child might make a potato print. The process was cheap and the ware was bright and attractive. Any young girl, just starting work at the pottery, could carry it out, using a bought-in, ready-cut sponge or one cut by the foreman. The ware was seldom marked and, on a coarse body, was destined for the cheapest markets. Thousands of pieces went to the urban poor, country dwellers and the colonies; in towns spongeware was often exchanged by the rag and bone man for worn out goods.

The process must not be confused, as it frequently is in the literature, with two others. From early times ordinary commercial sponges have been used to dab colour onto wares rather shapelessly; this is frequently seen on eighteenth century delft, for instance. 'Dabbing' like this can sometimes be confused with early examples of sponge-printing (where the pattern cut is fairly amorphous) but mature sponge-printing gives a totally different effect.

In the USA in particular, spongeware and spatterware are often coupled together and frequently confounded whereas they had quite different origins and often different markets. In spattering, the colour was in a dry, powdered form when applied to the ware by blowing or using oil. Both 'dabbing' and 'spattering' were carried out by experienced potters, male or female.

Sponge-printing spread quickly over the British Isles, though there is no evidence for it ever being used in Bristol or London. From Britain it was carried worldwide and was made, mostly in northern countries, from Russia to the USA until the 1930s when it disappeared from the industry.

Towards the end of the nineteenth century, spongeware was used in a rather different form to invade new markets. Several potteries began to make sponge-printed dishes, often also with hand-painted elements in the design, to serve the Asian market. India, Sri Lanka, Malaysia, Burma and Indonesia are countries where this ware was known and has now been recorded if not recovered. The trade was in the hands of British and Dutch potteries exclusively and three potteries in particular seem to have dominated it: the Glasgow Pottery of J. & M.P.Bell & Co.Ld., the Links Pottery of Kirkcaldy in Fife, and the Société Ceramiquê of Maastricht. Pieces have been recorded from other Scots (especially Verreville) and Dutch potteries and some English potteries including Adams and Spode, the latter having a large export to India in particular. This ware was different from the usual run of spongeware — the body was of higher quality and the decoration was more elaborate and more carefully carried out.

In the early 1990s there was a sudden revival of sponge-printing as a technique amongst British and Irish studio potters. This has now spread to more commercial works and the cheap and cheerful look of spongeware is again to be seen in many homes.

Pottery Descriptions: there are very few but they do not differ from the various potteries' usual marks.

Reading: Kelly, H.E. *Scottish Sponge-Printed Pottery* — Glasgow: Lomondside Press, 1992.

______. "The Export Trade of J. & M.P.Bell & Co. and other Scottish Potteries by H.E. Kelly" in *SPHR* 16 (1994): 49-57.

37.1. A selection of typical spongeware, all unattributable. Cow mug, 4" ht. (£60/$100); pink mug, 2.75" ht. (£45/$75); flow blue bowl, approx. 5" (£40/$70); large bowl, 8.75" diam. (£70/$120)

37.3. Irish potato bowl, so called because of dealers' descriptions. Almost certainly made in Scotland for the Irish market, 13.50" diam. (£200/$340).

37.5. Non-Scottish wares. Plate [English], 10.25" diam. (£45/$75); cockerel plate [Llanelly], 6.50" diam. (£90/$150); small bowl [Trenton, N.J.], 5.25" diam. (£20/$35); bowl [Maastricht], 6.75" diam. (£30/$50).

37.2. A selection of animal prints. The butterfly is from Clyde but the others are of unknown origin. Cow bowl, 10.25" diam. (£90/$150); reindeer bowl, 8.25" diam. (£70/$120); robin bowl, 6" diam. (£70/$120); butterfly, 5.50" diam. (£40/$70).

37.4. A selection of motto wares. The Welsh inscription bowl is from Llanelly Pottery, the others are unascribed. Football bowl, Christmas bowl, Welsh bowl, all 6.75" diam. (£60/$100, £60/100, £70/120). Jubilee mug, 4" ht. (£100/$170). Guid Morning plate, 7.25" diam. (£45/$75).

37.6. Patriotic wares: sherds of these have been found in many places in Scotland. It is certain that several potteries made this ware. Some may have been English. Mug, 3.50" ht. (£50/$85); Tipperary bowl, 6.75" diam. (£70/$120); Gordon Highlanders bowl (£100/$170).

38

Star Pottery, Glasgow

Apart from two paragraphs in Fleming, nothing original has been written about this Pottery and very little research has been done into its history. It was founded c.1878 by Johnstone Wardlaw junior, who had been a modeler at Britannia Pottery. Presumably he used his own savings to set up the Works, but he also borrowed £600 (approx. $1000) from his father, Johnstone Wardlaw senior, who was manager of Britannia Pottery.

The Pottery was built on the very northern edge of Glasgow, not far from the Possil Pottery and the industrial complex in which it stood. According to Fleming, the aim was to produce stilts and spurs for the Scottish potteries and there certainly was no other pottery supplying this need in Scotland at the time. Plumbago crucibles were also made and, certainly, commercial stoneware with a Bristol glaze and identical products with a Rockingham glaze. Fleming states that majolica was made but none has been identified.

After a short period, the Works was destroyed by fire, which went undetected until too late because of the pottery's situation. The Works was rebuilt in 1887 and is said to have made whiteware afterwards; but, within a year it was again completely destroyed by fire and never re-opened. No whiteware has ever been found.

Pottery Descriptions: impressed

J. Wardlaw Star Pottery

Star with a star.

38.1. Lidded storage jar with rouletted decoration, 7.25" ht. (£454/$75).

39

Verreville Pottery, Glasgow

The name Verreville means, of course, 'glass town' and the business began as a glassworks in 1777. It was built on the north bank of the Clyde in the village of Finnieston, at that time a holiday resort to the west of Glasgow, now well within the City.

In 1802 the works passed into the hands of John Geddes, who had been manager, and under him great changes were made, including the building of a pottery to the south of the glassworks. This land was bought in Christian Robertson's name (his wife). From the start, Geddes exported greatly to Ireland, Canada and the USA. A transfer-printed plate of 'Park Theatre, New York' is quite often met with for instance. Porcelain and earthenware were both made and decoration was by transfer print, hand painting, or sponge-printing.

In 1830 the Pottery, but not the Glassworks, was taken over by Robert Montgomery, who had been a clerk at the Pottery. He seems to have made much the same sort of goods as John Geddes, though very little has yet been recorded. This is not surprising since, on 8 June 1833, after less than three years as owner, Robert Montgomery was bankrupt.

The next owner was Robert A. Kidston, a trained potter who already owned the nearby Anderston Pottery and a glasswork. Under his management, the range of goods was greatly extended and the quality upgraded. Kidston's ambitions, however, outran the public's demand and in 1841 he, too, was bankrupted. At this time the pottery had two earthenware, two glost kilns, and one china biscuit and one glost kiln.

The estate was not settled until 1845 when, in circumstances yet to be fully clarified, the Pottery acquired five partners: Kidston, Robert Cochran, his brother Alexander, Charles Watson and Robert Goodwin. The most significant newcomers are the Cochran Brothers, who already had experience in running a pottery and a glasswork. Watson and Goodwin quickly disappeared, as did Kidston, and Robert Cochran was left as managing partner while Alexander ran the glassworks at the other end of the City.

Robert quickly dropped all the unprofitable lines made, leaving just white and coloured earthenwares . From then (c. 1845) until 1918, the pottery ran under three generations of Robert Cochrans, making earthenware for the home and overseas markets.

Since Robert Cochran senior and his descendants also ran the Britannia Pottery, the pottery descriptions are often similar and care should be taken.

The known wares of the Geddes period are all of transfer printed earthenware. Typical are plates with landscapes, often showing country houses (39.1), but mugs and plates were also made in transfer print, clobbered and sometimes with sponge-printing or pink lustre. Sometimes the name of the Works became part of the design (39.2). Mugs are known with views of Glasgow dockside. From the Montgomery period, only a few pieces of Willow have been found with his mark (39.3, 4).

This pattern is also known from the Kidston period (39.3) — sometimes, but not always, with the word Staffordshire attached to the usual backstamp (39.6). The range of wares made by Kidston had greatly expanded from previous periods. Soft paste porcelain tea wares with violet sprigs have been identified from excavation on the site, as have many transfer patterns in several colors (39.7). The sprigs on the porcelain and the 'hockey stick' mouldings, seem to be diagnostic (39.8). Commercial slipwares were, of course, made in abundance but are seldom found except in sherd form (39.5). Black basalte was certainly made but never marked.

United Kingdom is a changing pattern with at least five known centres, two of which show Edinburgh (one is misspelt) (39.3). A very elegant exotic landscape pattern called Lotus was made towards the end of this period. Pieces are found marked R.C. & Co. as well as K. & Co. (39.9).

Under Robert Cochran only white earthenware has been identified. Initially a very successful line was a range of octagonal pitchers. They carried transfers like Castile (a bullfight) or Olympian (kilted figures dancing) or were hand painted (39.10, 11, 12). Dinner wares were legion. Patterns include Australia and Genoa but Lotus was continued and Bells' Triumphal Car was copied. The most popular pattern, however, was a lacustrine landscape called Syria which remained in production throughout the rest of the pottery's life and was made also by Britannia Pottery (39.14).

In the late 1860s and 1870s, the pottery seems to have specialised in pitchers. New shapes were introduced and new patterns. One shape came into production as early as 1863 when it was used to celebrate the royal wedding of that year. The coat of arms of Glasgow made one very striking but unnamed pattern while another called Erin was presumably destined for Ireland or the Irish immigrants in western Scotland (39.15, 16). Pekin was another pattern shared with Britannia as well as with English potteries (39.17). At this time too, V.P. was often added to the pottery description in the backstamp to distinguish the wares from those of Britannia (39.18). Mona is a pattern used on dinner ware and pitchers (39.19).

In the 1880s again shapes and patterns changed. Straight-sided pitchers carried transfers that told a story like The Young Artist or The Donkey Ride (39.20, 21) or showed angels or the ever-popular sprigs of flowers (39.22). Dinner ware patterns became either very elaborate and vaguely 'Japanese' (39.21), floral (39.22) or wispy (39.20), though very plain hotel ware was made in some quantity (39.21). Spongeware was made throughout the life of the pottery but very little has been identified, though some of that was exported to Asia (39.23).

Verreville had a very varied existence under its different owners, but for over a hundred years it added some colorful pieces to the sum of Scottish pottery.

Pottery Descriptions: all printed.

John Geddes or JG
Verreville Pottery and Glass Company
M with a 'warranted' mark
RAK or RAK & Co.
R.C. & Co.
R.Cochran & Co.
R.C. & Co. V.P.

Reading: Kelly, H.E. "The Life of Robert Cochran of Verreville and Britannia Potteries" in *Scottish Industrial History* 18 (1996): 8-20.

Leishman, D.A. "The Anderston and Verreville Potteries and Glasswork" in *SPHR* 18 (1996): 3-14.

Quail, G. "The Verreville Pottery" in *SPHR* 8 (1984): 44-55.

Pattern List:

Many of the patterns on this list, particularly those from the Kidston period, are known only from sherds, so it is not always possible to give a complete description — or indeed any description at all. Most patterns from the Geddes period have no name.

Geddes period:

Japanese No.39
Park Theatre, New York — a townscape of a square with a central garden.

Montgomery period:

Willow

Kidston period:

Abbey
Agra — identical to the pattern of the same name made by Bell and Britannia.
Albert Sprig
Amboyna
Asiatic Pheasant — the usual.
Birds of Paradise — birds.
Chinese Pheasant — again a bird pattern with a very deep border.
Corinthian Flute
Cottage
Doric
Font
Fruit Basket
Grecian
Hong Kong — a landscape with cows — a porringer.
Lotus
Marine Grotto
Ottoman
Peruvian Hunters — landscape with hunters wearing feathers.
Pleasure Party — a lacustrine landscape, later renamed Picnic.
Rhine — the usual pattern
Syria

39.1. John Geddes plate (£250/$420).

Tudor
United Kingdom — several views are: Dublin, Dunkeld, Edinburgh, Edingburgh and Waterford.
Willow

Cochran period:
Anemone — floral
Apple Blossoms — apple blossoms
Aurora
Australia
Balmoral — two similar patterns
Bhamo — an export pattern — this may well be a Britannia pattern.
Bullfinch — a bird
Cadzow — a 'Japanese' pattern
Castile
Chinese — an oriental landscape
Clyde
Crystal Palace — another Exhibition commemorative.
Damascus — a lacustrine landscape
The Donkey Ride
Emerald
Empress
Erin
Exhibition — two patterns
Fairy
Florence — a changing lacustrine landscape
Game
Gardenia
Genoa
Gothic — a lacustrine landscape
Grecian
Lorne — pitcher for the 1871 royal wedding
Lotus
Mogul — an exotic procession
Mona
Nightingale — a bird
Olympian
Orchid — a toilet ware pattern of orchids with butterflies and birds.
Passion Flower — a passion flower
Pastoral — a 'Japanese' pattern.
Pekin
The Pet Lamb — a girl with a lamb
Picnic — same as Pleasure Party
The Plough Boy
Rose Mallow
Royal Mail
Rural
Seaweed — a curious pattern made up of a number of separate transfers, combined differently on each plate.
Shakspeare
Sir Garnet Wolsely
Stamboul — a lacustrine landscape
Star
Syria
Triumphal Car
Tyrol
Wellington — issued on Wellington's death
Wild Horse — scene with wild horses
Willow
Windsor — a floral abstract border
The Young Artist

39.2. Geddes mug (£600/$1000).

39.4. Montgomery mark.

39.3. Plates — back: Willow by Montgomery, 10" diam. and United Kingdom - Edinburgh by Kidston, 10.50" diam. — front: Willow, 10" diam. and Rhine, 9.5" diam. and pitchers, all by Kidston. Plates (£20-50/$35-85). Pitchers, 5.75" & 8.50"(£70/120 each).

39.6. Kidston mark.

39.5. Slipware sherds from Kidston period.

39.8. Diagnostic sprig.

39.7. Tea ware: soft paste porcelain with violet sprigs unmarked but Kidston period. Saucer, 6" diam. Tea set [six places] £100/$170.

39.9. Plate and platter: Lotus, 10.50" diam. & 17" lgth. (£45, 160/$75, 170). Bread plate: Exhibition, 11" diam. (£60/$100).

39.10. Pitchers: three with Castile, one with Grecian, 8.50" ht. (£40-50/$70-85).

39.11. Pitchers: Game, Olympian, 8" ht. (£40-50/$70-85).

39.12. Painted pitchers, 8" ht. (£40-50/$70-85).

39.14. Plates: Genoa, Syria, Australia, approx. 10.25" diam. (£20-45/$35-75).

39.13. Olympian mark.

39.15. Pitchers: Balmoral, Royal Wedding and Glasgow Arms, 7.50" & 8.50" ht. (£40-90/$70-150)

39.16. Pitcher: Erin, 8.50" ht. (£70/$120).

39.17. Pitchers: Pekin and Shakespeare, 6", 8", 8.50" ht. (£30-40/$50-70).

39.18. Mark of Glasgow Arms pitcher.

39.19. Plate, 10.25" diam. and pitcher, 8.50" ht.: Mona (£20, 35/$35, 60). Plate: Triumphal Car, 10.25" diam. (£30/$50).

39.20. Pitchers: The Young Artist, 8" ht, The Donkey Ride, 8" ht. (£120/$200). Plate: unnamed, 10" diam. (£20/$35). Toothbrush holder: Gardenia, 4" ht. (£20/$35).

39.21. Underdish: Empress, 12.75" lgth. (£20/$35). Plates: Tyrol, approx. 9" diam. (£45/$75), and hotel ware, 7.75" diam. (£10/$17). Pitcher: The Plough Boy, 7.75" ht. (£80/$135).

39.22. Pitchers — imperfect mark and Aurora, 7.75" ht. (£40/$70 each).

39.23. Spongeware plate: plates of this nature have been found in south east Asia, 8.75" diam. (£35/$60).

40

Victoria Pottery, Pollokshaws

The Victoria Pottery was founded in 1855 in the weaving village of Pollokshaws, south of Glasgow, but quickly thereafter absorbed into the City. The founding partners were David Lockhart and Charles Arthur. Lockhart came from Kirkcaldy in Fife, a pottery centre, but his family background was in the merchant class and what his connection with the pottery industry was is still unknown; Charles Arthur was at this time the manager of the Verreville Pottery in Glasgow.

They made earthenware decorated mainly with transfer prints, often carefully clobbered with enamels over the glaze; dinner wares, punch bowls and jugs were particularly featured and sponge-printing was used to a certain extent, again very carefully applied.

In 1865 Charles Arthur left to go to Bells' in Glasgow as their traveler, and David Lockhart carried on alone, making very similar, if slightly less upmarket, wares. Around 1876, however, the depression in trade caused a number of changes. Most of the old patterns were discontinued or at least became less popular and new patterns were brought in, the body coarsened and cream jugs and porringer sets became a marked feature. Large numbers of mugs were produced also.

In 1898 David Lockhart's two sons took over the works and, in order to stimulate sales, the wares became more and more patriotic, not to say jingoistic, with pattern names like Scotland Forever and Britannia Rules the Waves. But about 1911 a sudden silence ensued and nothing later has been certainly identified from the pottery. The Pottery closed down in 1953.

An album of posed photographs of the pottery at work, taken in 1896, is in the People's Palace Museum in Glasgow.

When set up in 1855, the Victoria Pottery clearly was aimed at capturing a share of the growing middle class market in the expanding city of Glasgow to which it had recently been joined by railroad. The wares made were largely dinner services and these proved very popular. In fact, judging by the number of extant pieces, the Pottery quickly achieved its aim. At this time there are found more pieces from this Pottery than from the much larger Britannia Pottery which was, of course, aiming for the trade in North and South America mainly.

The Lily and Rose pattern was very popular and has been reported in mulberry, grey and a very attractive lilac. It faded from popularity but was revived in the late 1870s in the much stronger colors favoured at that time (40.1). Country Scenery is a changing pattern whose central scenes vary from cows in a field to dramatic castles perched on crags (40.2). Other dinner ware patterns of the time include Anemone, Athens and the beautifully misspelt Pagado, later corrected to Pagoda (40.3).

Pitchers were, from the beginning, made in large numbers. One very elegant shape (40.7) was also made by several potteries in south Wales, so care must be taken in attributing unmarked pieces. Patterns range widely from scenes of everyday life — The Return from the Vineyard (40.3) — to allegorical figures — Persia (40.7). Clan Mackenzie may have been made for some specific occasion since it was very popular but was never followed up by pitchers for other clans. Commemorative pitchers include Sebastopol and The Alliance Jug, both of which were made during the Crimean War against Russia. A pattern virtually confined to this period is Virginia, a very delicate floral print found on mugs, pitchers, bedroom sets (i.e. ewers, basins, chamber pots, etc.) (40.9). In spite of its pattern name, it seems unlikely that this, or any other product of the Victoria Pottery, was destined for the U.S.A. The geographical position of the Pottery would have made an export trade rather awkward. Another peculiarity of Virginia is that it is always clobbered in several enamel colors. The clobbering is very carefully done, as it is in Persia (40.7), but it is uncommon in wares from this era in the Pottery's life.

The pattern which became the standard print of the Works and existed through a large part of its life is Etruscan, found in blue, brown and slate on a large assortment of goods, such as wall plaques and bedroom sets (40.5 & 6).

It is a curious fact that many potteries seem to have had one pattern that proved popular through most of its life. The supreme example is Bells' Triumphal Car but Verreville's Syria, Boness' Bosphorus, Methven's Verona and Fife's Milan all had a long and successful life.

The mark on Italian Fruit (40.8) shows a difficulty that several potteries experienced at this time with the new purple color that was to dominate the next fifteen or so years in Scots pottery history. The purple tended to separate into red and blue and to some extent the blue flowed through the glaze. In extreme examples it often looks as if the piece had been decorated with two prints, one in red and one in blue.

Also from this period, one marked example of spongeware has been identified. This is a wall plaque moulded with the head of Garibaldi and with the date 1863 and the name of the pottery in an incised inscription on the back. It is in the collection of Glasgow Museums and Art Galleries.

With the leaving of Charles Arthur, it is almost as if the pottery took on a new lease of life. This is probably a coincidence in that while Arthur hitched his wagon to a much bigger star, this happened just at the point when Victoria Pottery was reaping the benefit of ten years of producing very acceptable wares.

However that may be, the wares certainly change in several ways. While a few dinner sets are still in production, like Country Scenery and Anemone, the making of pitchers became much more important to the pottery, though punch bowls and mugs figure also. Besides this, clobbering becomes the norm now for transfer patterns.

Old pitcher shapes were retained, but with new patterns like Sèvres and Arab (40.10), but these were quickly printed also onto new shapes. These were also printed with a speciality of Victoria Pottery, pictures of boys with dogs. This must have been a best selling theme since no less than three such prints appear at this time: Innocence, Greyhound, and Charlie. In the last of these, a boy is teaching his dog to kill rats, watched from a nearby wall by a cat. Charlie proved so popular that it is found also on mugs and punch bowls, as is Innocence.

An interesting set of wares, identified by shape since they are never marked, is shown in photo 40.13. The punchbowl shows four vignettes of the seasons and two others which are not named here but are elsewhere as Feeding Poultry and Returning from Market. These six are found in various combinations also on pitchers, mugs and porringers. The most probable reason for their never being marked is that the plates for the transfers were bought in from one of the English firms which specialised in this trade.

Many new patterns were appearing in this period. Palermo is found on pitchers and punch bowls, as are Glencoe, Richmond and Cuba (40.14, 15, 17). Venice proved less successful and has been found only on porringers up till now. Java is first found at this time but continues into the next period (40.18). The mark for Greyhound shows that the difficulties experienced with purple had been overcome.

Victory, Antelopes and Golden Eagle are other new pitcher patterns (40.21). One commemorative was made — for the royal wedding of 1863 (40.23). Some patterns, as we have seen, are bought in and this includes sheet patterns (40.22), one of which is found also on pieces by Bo'ness. Amber lustre, particularly in combination with sepia is used as a transfer or sponge print. Some spongeware with this combination has been identified by shape (40.16). Bowls and mugs are also found (40.22-23).

The wares of the second period are certainly aimed slightly lower in the market than those of Lockhart & Arthur but around 1876 the aim is lowered still more. At this time the wares are changed considerably. Most old patterns and shapes are scrapped and new ones designed. Dinner wares are not completely abandoned, as is shown by Bothnia (40.26), but, on the other hand, Brussels seems meant more as a wall plaque than a practical dinner plate. Pitcher shapes change again to follow the fashion of the times. Straight-sided shapes are favoured in patterns like Oban, Derwent (40.27), Rothsay, Kensington and Fidelity (40.25), the last another boy and dog print. A Christmas pitcher is also found at this time, one of only two known from this Pottery; it is Felicity (40.24). The only 'wrap around' pattern also appeared now — Loch Fyne (40.25). Orient and Avon introduce a new spiral shape of pitcher (40.26). An innovation of this time which proved immensely popular was the bowl with straight sides (40.27-30). This is still found from this and the following period in amazing numbers and a vast array of transfers. Some were produced for royal jubilees or Glasgow Exhibitions (40.27), some for Christmas greetings (40.28), but many simply had a pattern and motto that would appeal to the workers of the village of Pollokshaws and of Glasgow. They were usually sold either in pairs as porringers or combined with a small creamer as a milk and sugar set. They were very popular at the time and are still so with collectors.

A very large find of mugs from the pottery was made some years ago in a large house in the Hebrides. Although over a hundred mugs were found, only four patterns were represented and one of those was present in small quantity (40.23, 30). In fact Yarmouth (40.30, 31) is really only one pattern though found in two very different forms on different mugs. One shows a rowing boat in a harbour, the other a pile of dead fish, but the two scenes are also found on the same bowl. A polychrome transfer found on other mugs and wall plaques shows two peasant children. It is called Youth (40.30). Another wall plaque — Life Buoy — has, as well as a clobbered print, dabbing in gold and blue (40.30).

In its final period, the pottery was battling for life. Victoria's first solution to the problem was to sink into a degree of patriotism bordering on jingoism. Bowls appeared with thistles and tartan (40.29) and with mottoes like 'Britannia Rules the Waves' (40.32) or 'Scotland Forever'. Our Heroes (40.32) shows three generals from the Boer War. Purity shows two girls at the village pump (40.32). Pitchers of this period are rather scarce. They show the influence of Art Nouveau — Verona — or commemorate royal events — Queen (40.33). In fact there seem to be several contemporary patterns all called Queen. One 'wrap around' pattern — The Water Carrier (40.33) — is found on pitchers and punchbowls and it and Elephant were made for export to South East Asia.

About 1911, the wares of Victoria Pottery disappear completely. Since the pottery worked on until the 1950s, this is puzzling. The solution seems to be that during all that time they made unmarked plain white ware. In the postwar period, this seems to have dwindled into just white chamber pots — a sad end to the life of an enterprising pottery which had produced wares of great charm.

Pottery Descriptions: all transfer prints

Lockhart & Arthur and L. & A., both 1855-1864
Lockhart & Co. and L. & Co., both 1865-c.1876
D.L. & Co., c.1876-1898
D.L. & S. 1898 onwards.

Reading: Kelly, H.E. "The Jugs of the Victoria Pottery" in *SPHR* 11 (1987): 10-22.
______. "The Wares of the Victoria Pottery" in *SPHR* 14 (1992): 16-38.
King, Elspeth. "Pollokshaws Pottery Photographs" in *SPHR* 12 (1988): 31-49.

Pattern List:

a) Lockhart & Arthur — L. & A. — 1855-1864

The Alliance Jug — uniformed figures and scroll with To the Brave Soldiers and Sailors of the Crimea.
Anemone
Athens
Bird's Nest
Clan Mackenzie
Country Scenery
Etruscan
Fibre — the usual pattern of this name
Fountain — a fountain scene
Hawthorn
Italian Fruit
Lily and Rose
Pagado — Pagoda
The Return from the Vineyard
Rhine — the classic pattern
Sebastopol
Sèvres
Virginia
Willow — the usual pattern.

b) Lockhart & Co. — L. & Co. — 1865-c.1876

Arab
Batavia
Ceylon — a scatter of flowers.
Charlie
Country Scenery
Cuba
Etruscan
Glencoe
Golden Eagle
Grecian — the usual sponge print in grey — unmarked, known from shape.
Greyhound
Hawthorn
Innocence
Java
Millport — a frog mug with a blue landscape print.

40.1. Lily and Rose including the later revival. Tureen and underdish, 15" diam. (£160/$270); platter, 17.50" lgth. (£160/$270); punchbowl, 9" diam. (£70/$120); bowl, 5.25" diam. (£25/$40).

Oriental
Palermo
Persia
Peru — punch bowl with lacustrine landscape.
Richmond
Roseneath
Sèvres
Sheepshearing — men shearing sheep.
Venice
Victory

c) D.L. & Co. — c.1876-1898

Abbotsford — children with dogs and a goat
Alva — a ribbon tied in a bow.
Antelopes
Ballater
Balmoral — Queen Victoria and her residences.
Blair Athole — scene with birds in trellises.
Bothnia
Braemar
Britania (sic)
Brussels
Burns — Burns' head.
Caledonia — thistles, rose, shamrocks.
Canada — children sledging — a Christmas pitcher.
Daliah (sic) — a dahlia
Dalmeny — floral design on mug.
Derwent
Etruscan
Felicity
Fidelity
Fleetwood
Glasgow Exhibition 1888
Gleniffer — birds on twigs.
Glenrosa — an elf and dancing figures.
Glenshee
Harp — a woman playing a harp in a landscape.
Herbert — a boy lying by a stream.
Inchrye — pansies and foliage.
Kensington
Kilsyth — a horse throwing a hunts man.
King and Queen — busts — made for coronation of Edward VII and Alexandra.
King William
Life Buoy
Lily and Rose
Lily of the Valley
Lochee
Melrose — a bird on a bough.
Moffat — floral.
Oban
Orient
Oriental — brought back from Java.
Prince — Prince Charlie.
Queen
Rose
Rothsay
Sicily — a hand with a basket of fruit.
Singapore — two oriental figures and a peacock.
Sultana — floral
Sweet Home — fence with birds and motto HOME SWEET HOME.
Tartan — a stripe of tartan.
Thistle
Waverley — overall star and floral shapes.
Yarmouth

d) D.L. & S. — 1898-c.1953

Auld Lang Sync — with motto on bowl
Britania (sic)
Cattle — scene with cattle.
Elephant — three men in a howdah on an elephant.
Exhibition (1901) — a view of the Glasgow Exhibition.
Holly
King and Queen
Kinross
Our Heroes
Purity
Scotland Forever — thistles.
Thistle
Thrift — an old woman spinning yarn in front of a cottage.
Verona
The Water Carrier
Youth

40.2. Platter and plates of Country Scenery, Oriental in black. Platter, 16" lgth. (£140/$235); plates, 9.25" & 9.75" diam. (£30/$50).

40.3. Plates: Athens, 9.50" diam., Pagado, 9.25" diam. (£30/50); platter: Anemone, 17.50" lgth. (£120/$200): pitcher: The Return from the Vineyard, 8.50" ht. (£90/$150).

40.4. Mark on wares in 40.3.

40.5. Etruscan — an early wall plaque, 10.75" diam. (£130/$220) and later basin, 14.50" diam. (£50/$85).

40.6. Etruscan — ewer (£50/$85).

40.7. Pitchers: Clan Mackenzie, 7.75" ht., Persia (clobbered and plain), 8.75" ht., Italian Fruit, 8.75" ht., Sebastopol, 8.75" ht. (£90-170/$150-280).

40.8. Mark on Italian Fruit.

40.9. Pitchers: Virginia, 8.50" ht. and much later King William, 8" ht. (see 40.29) (£90-120/$150-200).

40.10. Pitchers: Sèvres, 8.75" ht., Arab, 9" ht., both in two shapes (£90/$150 each).

40.12. Mark on Greyhound.

40.11. Boys and dogs: Innocence (x 2), Greyhound and Charlie as pitcher and mug. Pitchers, 9" ht. (£90-100/$150-170); mug, 4.75" diam. (£70/$120).

40.13. Bought-in transfers. Pitcher, 9" ht. and punch bowl, 10.25" diam. (£70/$120 each); mugs, 3.50" & 2.75" diam. (£60/$100 each).

40.14. Pitchers: Bird's Nest, unnamed, Glencoe, Cuba, 8.75" ht. (£60-90/$100-150).

40.15. Bowl: Roseneath, 5.25" diam. (£25/$40). Punch bowl: Palermo, 10.25" diam. (£80/$135). Pitchers: Richmond, 9" ht. (£90/$150 each).

40.16. Spongeware: unmarked, identified by shape. Punch bowl, 10" diam. (£80/$135), pitcher, 8" ht. (£45/$75), bowls, 4.50", 4.75" ht. (£30/$50)

40.17. Punchbowl: Heather, 10" diam. (£80/135). Porringer: Venice, approx. 6" diam. (£25/$40). Pitcher: Palermo, 9" ht. (£80/$135).

40.18. Pitchers: Java, Braemar, Lily of the Valley, 8" ht. (£90/$150). Porringers: Rose (D.L.& Co.) and unnamed (L. & Co.), 5.25" diam. (£50/$85)

40.19. Pitcher, sponge-printed, unmarked but identified from shape, 8" ht. (£45/$75).

40.20. Mark from Etruscan.

40.21. Pitchers: Java, Victory, Batavia and unmarked pitcher with amber lustre, approx. 8.25" ht. (£40-90/$70-150).

40.22. Pitchers, 8" ht. and bowls with bought in transfers, no marks (£20-50/$35-85). Bowl, approx. 4" diam. with blue ground for Glasgow Exhibition 1888 (£20/$35).

40.23. Pitchers: for royal wedding (1863), Golden Eagle, Antelopes, 8" ht. (£90-100/$150-170). Mug: unnamed but L. & Co., 3" diam. (£50/$85).

40.24. Plate: Brussels, 9.50" diam. (£60/$100). Pitchers: Felicity (at top), 9" ht., Oban, 7.25" ht., Derwent, 7.75" ht. (£90/$150 each).

40.25. Pitchers: Rothsay, 7" ht., Kensington, 8" ht., Loch Fyne, 6.75" ht., Fidelity, 8" ht. (£90-100/$150-170).

40.26. Serving dish: Bothnia, 16.50" lgth. (£60/$100). Pitchers: Orient, 6.25" ht., Avon, 8" ht. (£80-90/$135-150). Porringer: Glenshee, 5.50" diam. (£20/$35).

40.27. Porringers: Glasgow Exhibition 1888, Queen, Britania, 5.25" diam. (£50/$85). Creamer: Queen but a different pattern, 4" ht. (£35/$60).

40.28. Two Christmas bowls and a sugar and cream set, 5.25" diam.: Holly (D.L. & Co.) bowls (£55/$90); set (£70/$120).

40.29. Porringers: Fleetwood, Thistle, 5.25" diam. (£40/$70). Creamer: Ballater, 4" ht. (£35/$60). Plate: King William, 9.75" diam. (£50/$85). These are never marked but can be securely attributed to Victoria Pottery.

40.30. Mugs: Youth, 3" diam. and two forms of Yarmouth, 4" diam. (£40/$70). Wall plaque: Life Buoy, 10" diam. (£50/$85).

40.31. Porringer: Inchrye, approx. 5" diam. (£35/$60). Moulded pitcher with amber lustre, approx. 8" ht. (£30/$50).

40.32. Bowls: Britania, Our Heroes, Kinross, 5.25" diam. (£50/$85). Creamer: Purity, 4" ht. (£30/$50).

40.33. Pitchers: Queen, The Water Carrier, Verona, approx. 8" ht. (£40-90/$70-150).

Wellington Pottery, Glasgow

Virtually no research has gone into the history of this Pottery since the publication of Fleming's *Scottish Pottery* in 1923.

It was established in 1797 in the east end of Glasgow to use local clays to make redware; redware potteries were a rarity in Glasgow. Flower pots and garden ornaments were the staple products. In 1830 it was taken over by Adam Cubie, a potter from Prestonpans and in 1844, after Cubie's death, John Williamson was the proprietor. He was Cubie's son-in-law. The Pottery continued in the Williamson family, John being succeeded by his son, A.C.Williamson, in 1864.

William Clough may have been the manager or a partner. He was a nephew of Bells' original manager, Robert Clough. He had come from Yorkshire with his uncle and had unsuccessfully run the Ladyburn Pottery in Greenock in partnership with a member of the Geddes family. The partnership lasted for less than a year.

About 1894 the business was sold to Austin & McDonald who moved it to North Canal Bank Street, Port Dundas, on the banks of the Forth & Clyde Canal where coal could be imported from Monklands and wares exported to either side of Scotland. The Pottery closed in 1934.

Very few pieces, apart from ordinary flower pots, have been identified from this Pottery, though various slip-trailed wares have been attributed to it and it is known from catalogues that a variety of other wares were made.

Pottery Descriptions — both impressed: Wellington Pottery
Williamson Wellington Pottery

41.1. Crocus pot in the form of an elephant — red clay, white clay added as eyes and tusks — 9.50 lgth. (£45/$75). Impressed WELLINGTON POTTERY GLASGOW.

42

West Pans Pottery, East Lothian

By 1764 William Littler, a bankrupt English potter, had established himself in business as a china manufacturer in West Pans on the coast, east of Edinburgh. There is some discussion of which wares Littler made at Longton Hall, where he had been working, and which he made at West Pans; however, he certainly used local cobalt ores in Scotland to produce an intense but not completely controllable blue decoration on his ware. He was bankrupted anew in 1774.

There is a hiatus of ten years either in the working of the pottery at this time or in our knowledge. The next known owner is Robert Bagnell, an English potter who had already been concerned in making pottery in Glasgow and been bankrupted in dramatic circumstances in 1782. He took as a partner Anthony de la Chapelle. The product was probably creamware but no marked pieces are known and much seems to have been exported to France. The Pottery worked until 1792 when difficulties led to another bankruptcy.

The Works were now converted to the manufacture of stoneware and run by the West Pans Stone Ware Co., quickly followed by J. Read & Co. By March 1794, Robert Bagnell seems to have returned accompanied by William Webster, also a potter. In 1796 we have the dissolution of owners Cockson, Jardine & Co., though it is possible that William Cockson and Robert Jardine carried on after this date.

At some time William Smith took control and went bankrupt in 1808. The Pottery now remained empty until 1815 when it reopened for the making of stoneware and redware. David Wilson took over then, followed by Smils, Wilson & Co. in 1816 but internal disputes among the partners again led to bankruptcy in 1817. During its last two periods, the pottery was run as Roger & Davidson and then Roger & Co. for the making of redware. No marked products are known from any period. The Pottery finally closed c.1840.

Reading: Kelly, H.E. "West Pans" and "Notes on two East Lothian Potteries" in *Northern Ceramic Society Newsletter* 88 (1992): 30-34.

McVeigh, P. *Scottish East Coast Potteries 1750-1840.* Edinburgh

Quail, G. "Wm. Littler & West Pans China Works" in *NCS Newsletter* 44 (1981): 10-27.

______. "The Bagnell & Co. period of West Pans" in *NCS Newsletter* 62 (1986): 5-13.

______. "The Later Period of West Pans Pottery" in *NCS Newsletter* 63 (1986): 16-21.

______. "The Rogers & Davidson & Rogers & Co. period of West Pans" in *NCS Newsletter* 64 (1986): 38-42.

Turnbull, J. "West Pans — the W.Smith, Wilson, Gibson, Smils Partnership" in *NCS Newsletter* 96 (1994): 30-34.

Pots at the Pans — catalogue — Newtongrange (1990)

43 Glossary

Ashet: this is peculiarly Scots. It derives from the French word assiette and means the sub-rectangular dish used to serve meat at the table. Standard English seems to have no word for this and in the literature one often sees "meat plate," which is unsatisfactory. I am told that "platter" is used in at least some areas of the U.S.A.

Biscuit: the state of a pot which has been fired once but has not yet been glazed. Its surface will be rough and absorbent

Body: the blend of raw materials from which a pot is made.

Bristol Glaze: a glaze often used on stoneware. It contains feldspar and largely replaced salt glazing.

Changing Pattern: Used in this book to mean a transfer pattern with a constant border but a central scene which varies with the shape of the piece. The classic Scots pattern is Triumphal Car.

Clobbering: painting in enamels above the glaze to color parts of a transfer pattern.

Japanese Pattern: a pattern made up of disparate elements arrange assymetrically. They were inspired by Japanese art and were very popular in the last quarter of the nineteenth century.

Jug: used in Britain to denote what in the U.S.A. is called a pitcher.

Mocha: a method of decoration in which a slip is applied to a pot and soured with a "tea" made often with old tobacco juice or stale urine. Used particularly on beer mugs in the nineteenth century.

Pig: old Scots word for pottery; still often used to mean a stoneware hot water bottle. A pirley pig means a penny bank in ceramic.

Pitcher: see jug

Platter: see ashet

Plumbago: a body containing fireclay and graphite often used to make crucibles for high temperature furnaces

Porringer: a bowl from which oatmeal porridge is eaten in nineteenth century Scotland; the poorer classes often ate all their food from these rather than from plates, especially in rural areas.

Quaich: a shallow bowl with two horizontal handles. Traditionally used for whisky drinking, it is now mainly ceremonial or decorative.

Rockingham Glaze: a brown manganese glaze used for teapots and other kitchen wares.

Sagger: a fireclay box used to hold pottery during firing in the kiln to protect it from direct flame.

Sgraffito: a method of decorating a pot by scratching through an applied slip to reveal a different color underneath.

Slip: a mixture of clay and water. Ware decorated with this is referred to as slipware.

Slip Moulding: a method of making hollowware. A plaster of Paris mould is filled with slip. The plaster absorbs water from the slip, causing the clay nearest the plaster to solidify gradually. When the clay reaches the required thickness, the rest of the slip is decanted. On drying, the pot is easily removed from the mould.

Traveler: the salesman for a pottery. In Victorian Scotland, the traveler was a very important person, sometimes a partner, who made long trips all over Britain and Ireland to obtain orders.

Splash Glaze: a method of decoration in which several colors of glaze are used on different parts of a pot. It was very popular in the late nineteenth century with majolica potteries and fireclay potteries.

Trio: a modern dealers' term for a teacup, saucer and plate resulting from a broken up teaset.